Computer accounting systems

Workbook

Tara Askham

Published by Osborne Books Limited
Unit 1B Everoak Estate
Bromyard Road, Worcester WR2 5HP
Tel 01905 748071
Email books@osbornebooks.co.uk
Website www.osbornebooks.co.uk

Design by Laura Ingham

Printed by CPI Group (UK) Limited, Croydon, CR0 4YY, on environmentally friendly, acid-free paper from managed forests.

British Library Cataloguing in Publication Data
A catalogue record for this book is available from the British Library

ISBN 978 1909173 583

Contents

Introduction

Acknowledgements

The publisher wishes to thank the following for their help with the reading and production of the book: Jon Moore, Bee Pugh and Cathy Turner. Thanks are also due to Hania Lee for her technical reading and to Laura Ingham for her designs for this series.

The publisher is indebted to the Association of Accounting Technicians for its help and advice to our author and editors during the preparation of this text.

Author

Tara Askham worked in the accountancy profession for a number of years before training to be a lecturer. She has been AAT Coordinator at Central College, Nottingham, and currently works for the International Association of Bookkeepers as a freelance examiner. She has written examination papers for both the National Qualifications Framework and Qualifications and Credit Framework for Bookkeeping and has wide experience in writing assessments for computerised testing. Tara is a consultant to the AAT, writing and reviewing assessments and contributing to the Standards.

Introduction

what this book covers

This book has been written specifically to cover the 'Computerised accounting' Unit which is mandatory for the AAT Level 2 Certificate in Accounting and the AAT Level 2 Diploma in Accounting and Business.

The Sage system (Version 18) has been chosen as it is widely used both by businesses and by training providers.

what this book contains

This book provides four full Practice Assessments to prepare the student for the Computer Based Assessments. They are based directly on the structure, style and content of the sample assessment material provided by the AAT at www.aat.org.uk. Suggested answers to the Practice Assessments are set out in this book.

further information

If you want to know more about our products and resources, please visit www.osbornebooks.co.uk for further details and access to our online shop.

Practice
assessment 1
Frances Fireplaces

Instructions to candidates

This assessment asks you to input data into a computerised accounting package and produce documents and reports. There are 14 tasks and it is important that you attempt all tasks.

The time allowed to complete this computerised accounting assessment is **2 hours**.

Additional time up to a maximum of 1 hour may be scheduled by your tutor to allow for delays due to computer issues such as printer queues.

It is important that you print **all** reports and documents specified in the tasks so your work can be assessed. A checklist has been provided at the end of the assessment to help you check that all documents and reports have been printed.

If your computerised accounting system allows for the generation of PDFs, these can be generated instead of hard copy prints. Screenshots saved as image files are also acceptable.

Data

Frances Fireplaces is an existing business that supplies bespoke fireplaces to the local area. The owner is **Frances Webster,** who operates as a sole trader.

The business has previously kept manual books but from **1 Oct 20XX**, the accounts are to be computerised.

You are employed as an accounts assistant.

You can assume that all documentation has been checked for accuracy and authorised by Frances Webster.

Cash and credit sales are analysed in **two** ways:

*   Gas fires

*   Electric fires

Some nominal ledger accounts have already been allocated account codes. You may need to amend account names or create other account codes.

The business is registered for VAT (Standard Accounting). The rate of VAT charged on all goods and services sold by Frances Fireplaces is 20%.

All expenditure should be analysed as you feel appropriate.

Before you start you should:

*   Set the financial year to start on **1 October of the current year**.

*   Set the software date as **31 October of the current year**.

*   Set up the company details by entering the name **Frances Fireplaces** and the address: **24 Steinbeck Street, Firtown, East Beeston, FW6 3RB**. In a training environment you should add your name after the business name to identify your printouts.

Task 1

(a) Set up customer records for each of the customers below, with opening balances as at 1 October 20XX.

(b) Generate a customer activity report on screen. Check it for accuracy and, if necessary, correct any errors. You do not need to print the customer activity report.

Customer name and address	Contact name and number	Customer account code	Opening balance as at 1 October 20XX	Payment terms	Credit limit
Cranthorne Interiors 124 Cranthorne Street Gilford GC26 1TU	Habibe Mahmood 0162 748542	CRA001	£4,304.40	30 days	£5,000.00
Homeware Showroom 23A Stone Street Gilford GC22 7BY	Claire Hemmingway 0162 147526	HOM001	£650.50	30 days	£25,000.00
Shirley Styles Unit 24 Teabrook Industrial Estate Beeston BE4 9AL	Phillip Sandford 0178 264240	SHI001	£1,670.00	30 days	£28,000.00

Task 2

(a) Set up supplier records for each of the suppliers below, with opening balances as at 1 October 20XX.

(b) Generate a supplier activity report on screen. Check it for accuracy and, if necessary, correct any errors. You do not need to print the supplier activity report.

Supplier name and address	Contact name and number	Supplier account code	Opening balance as at 1 October 20XX	Payment terms	Credit limit
Chris Carrington Ltd 9A Gedling Lane Beeston BC4 6PY	Mark Carrington 0178 364214	CHR001	£980.00	30 days	£2,500.00
East Town Electrics 198 Grange Avenue Wilford WS7 2CS	Seema Tomlinson 0191 471256	EAS001	£2,876.50	30 days	£8,000.00
Mark Sharpe 64 Milford Rise Gilford GC14 8LA	Mark Sharpe 0162 589301	MAR001	£940.55	30 days	£3,500.00

Task 3

(a)   Using the list of nominal ledger balances below, set up nominal ledger records for each account. Select, amend or create nominal ledger codes where required.

(b)   Generate a trial balance on screen. Check it for accuracy and, if necessary, correct any errors. You do not need to print the trial balance.

List of nominal ledger accounts as at 1 October 20XX

Account name	Debit £	Credit £
Bank	16,000.00	
Petty cash	160.00	
Office equipment	15,400.00	
Motor vehicles	32,360.00	
Sales ledger control account*	6,624.90	
Purchases ledger control account*		4,797.05
VAT on sales		7,420.60
VAT on purchases	3,930.00	
Capital		15,700.00
Drawings**	2,000.00	
Sales – Gas fires		35,653.37
Sales – Electric fires		16,923.44
Goods for resale	4,019.56	
Totals	**80,494.46**	**80,494.46**

*   As you have already entered opening balances for customers and suppliers you may not need to enter these balances

** You may need to set up an account for drawings

Task 4

Using the information from the sales day book and sales returns day book below, enter these transactions into the computer.

Summary of sales invoices

Date 20XX	Customer	Invoice number	Gross	VAT	Net	Gas fires	Electric fires
2 October	Shirley Styles	280	16,648.80	2,774.80	13,874.00	13,874.00	
10 October	Homeware Showroom	281	21,009.60	3,501.60	17,508.00	12,908.00	4,600.00
	Totals		37,658.84	6,276.40	31,382.00	26,782.00	4,600.00

Summary of sales credit notes

Date 20XX	Customer	Credit note number	Gross	VAT	Net	Gas fires	Electric fires
12 October	Cranthorne Interiors	67	84.00	14.00	70.00		70.00
14 October	Shirley Styles	68	1,944.00	324.00	1,620.00	1,620.00	
	Totals		2,028.00	338.00	1,690.00	1,620.00	70.00

Task 5

Enter the following purchase invoices and purchase credit note into the computer.

Purchase Invoice

INVOICE

East Town Electrics

198 Grange Avenue, Wilford, WS7 2CS
VAT registration number 748 5462 35

FAO Frances Webster
Frances Fireplaces
24 Steinbeck Street
Firtown
East Beeston
FW6 3RB

invoice no   745226

date   13 October 20XX

Supply of goods for resale	£3,740.00
goods total	**£3,740.00**
VAT @ 20%	**£748.00**
TOTAL	**£4,488.00**

Purchase Credit note

CREDIT NOTE

East Town Electrics

198 Grange Avenue, Wilford, WS7 2CS
VAT registration number 748 5462 35

Frances Fireplaces
24 Steinbeck Street
Firtown
East Beeston
FW6 3RB

credit note no CN541

date   17 October 20XX

Goods for resale returned	£47.00
goods total	**£47.00**
VAT @ 20%	**£9.40**
TOTAL	**£56.40**

Purchase Invoice

INVOICE

Chris Carrington Limited

9A Gedling Lane, Beeston, BC4 6PY
VAT registration number 851 6874 74

invoice to

Frances Fireplaces
24 Steinbeck Street
Firtown
East Beeston
FW6 3RB

invoice no	**0014582**
date	**25 October 20XX**

Repairs to the showroom	£876.00
VAT @ 20%	£175.20
Total invoice	£1,051.20

Task 6

Enter the following customer receipts from the documents below.

BACS REMITTANCE ADVICE

TO

Frances Fireplaces
24 Steinbeck Street
Firtown
East Beeston
FW6 3RB

FROM

Shirley Styles
Unit 24
Teabrook Industrial Estate
Beeston
BE4 9AL

Date 26 October 20XX

Your ref	Our ref	Amount
O/bal	INV2366	£1,670.00
		Total £1,670.00

THIS HAS BEEN PAID BY BACS CREDIT TRANSFER DIRECTLY TO YOUR BANK ACCOUNT

Gilford Bank plc
285 High Street
Gilford, GJ7 5RD

Date *26 October 20XX*

Frances Fireplaces

Four thousand, two hundred and twenty pounds and forty pence

£ 4,220.40

A/c payee only

Habibe Mahmood

203654   47858765   10-24-89   Cranthorne Interiors

NB: This cheque pays the balance as at 1 October less credit note 67

Newford Bank
36 High Street
East Beeston, BE6 8RN

Date *28 October 20XX*

Frances Fireplaces

Two thousand pounds only

£ 2,000.00

A/c payee only

Claire Hemmingway

632012   78426598   26-04-62   Homeware Showroom

NB: This cheque is a payment on account

Task 7

(a)   Enter the following payments to suppliers into the computer.

Payments to suppliers

Date (20XX)	Supplier	Type	£	Details
20 October	East Town Electrics	Cheque 020142	2,820.10	Pays balance as at 1 October less credit note CN541
24 October	Mark Sharpe	BACS	940.55	Pays balance as at 1 October

(b)   Print a remittance advice for the payment to East Town Electrics.

Task 8

(a) You have received the following email. Enter this transaction into the computer.

Email	
To:	Accounts Assistant
From:	Frances Webster
Date:	16 October 20XX
Subject:	Vehicle Insurance

Hello

Today I have renewed the vehicle insurance on two of our company vehicles. The amount totalled £1,490.60 and I have paid it using the business debit card.

Please record this transaction. VAT is not applicable.

Kind regards

Frances

(b) You have received the following email. Enter this transaction into the computer.

Email	
To:	Accounts Assistant
From:	Frances Webster
Date:	17 October 20XX
Subject:	Transfer between bank accounts

Hello

Today I have completed an online transfer to transfer £10,000 from the bank current account into the bank deposit account.

Please record this transaction. VAT is not applicable.

Kind regards

Frances

(c) Enter the following cash sales receipts into the computer.

Frances Fireplaces		Receipt No: 56
		date 29 October 20XX

description		£	p
X2 Gas fires		434	40
Total (Including VAT @ 20%)		434	40

VAT reg no. 578 3645 63

Frances Fireplaces		Receipt No: 57
		date 29 October 20XX

description	£	p
X4 Gas fires	724	00
X1 Electric fires	146	00
	870	00
VAT @ 20%	174	00
Total	1,044	00

VAT reg no. 578 3645 63

Task 9

Refer to the standing order schedule below.

(a)   Set up recurring entries for the transactions below.

(b)   Print a screenshot of the screen setting up each of the recurring entries.

(c)   Process the first payment for each standing order.

Details	Amount	Frequency	Total number of payments	Payment start date 20XX
STO receipt for rental income from S Shaw	£600.00 plus VAT	Monthly	6	1 October
STO payment for rates to Gilford Council	£142.00 (VAT Exempt)	Monthly	12	5 October

Task 10

(a)   A petty cash reimbursement request has been received for £40.00 to restore the petty cash account to £200.00. Enter a transfer from the bank account to the petty cash account for this amount using cheque number 020141 dated 1 October 20XX.

(b)   Enter the following petty cash vouchers into the computer.

---

petty cash voucher   Number *101*

                                          date   *17 Oct 20XX*

description		amount
	£	p
Postage stamps (VAT not applicable)	*8*	*60*
	8	*60*
Receipt attached		

---

petty cash voucher   Number *102*

                                          date   *18 Oct 20XX*

description		amount
	£	p
Envelopes	*12*	*00*
VAT	*2*	*40*
Total	*14*	*40*
Receipt attached		

---

petty cash voucher   Number *103*

                                          date   *18 Oct 20XX*

description		amount
	£	p
Ink for printer (VAT included)	*16*	*50*
	16	*50*
Receipt attached		

Task 11

Enter the following journals into the computer.

Journal entry 061 30 October 20XX	Dr	Cr
Wages	1,000.00	
Drawings		1,000.00
Correction of posting error. Wages incorrectly posted to drawings.		

Journal entry 062 30 October 20XX	Dr	Cr
Bank	18.00	
General rates		18.00
An error in the amount shown on the standing order schedule for general rates.		

Task 12

Refer to the following bank statement.

(a)   Enter the bank charges (no VAT) which have not yet been accounted for.

(b)   Reconcile the bank statement. If the bank statement does not reconcile, check your work and make the necessary corrections.

GILFORD BANK PLC

Statement of account

Gilford Bank plc
285 High Street
Gilford
GJ7 5RD

Account
Frances Fireplaces
24 Steinbeck Street
Firtown
East Beeston
FW6 3RB   Date: 31 October 20XX

Date	Details	Debit £	Credit £	Balance £
01-Oct	Opening balance			16,000.00 C
01-Oct	STO Rent S Shaw		720.00	16,720.00 C
05-Oct	STO Gilford Council	124.00		16,596.00 C
05-Oct	020141	40.00		16,556.00 C
17-Oct	Transfer from 102745874	10,000.00		6,556.00 C
18-Oct	Debit card	1,490.60		5,065.40 C
26-Oct	BACS Shirley Styles		1,670.00	6,735.40 C
26-Oct	Credit 203475		4,220.40	10,955.80 C
27-Oct	020142	2,820.10		8,135.70 C
27-Oct	BACS Mark Sharpe	940.55		7,195.15 C
30-Oct	Bank charges	23.60		7,171.55 C
	D = Debit C = Credit			

Task 13

(a) Use the password 'FRANw614' to protect your accounting data and print a screenshot showing the entry of the password into the computer.

If it is not possible to enter the password given in the assessment, print a screenshot showing the entry of your own password (eg at the login stage).

(b) Back up your work to a suitable storage medium using a filename made up of your name followed by FFbackup. For example if your name is Ellie Shipstone the filename would be 'EllieShipstoneFFbackup'. Print a screenshot of the backup screen showing the location of the backup data.

If it is not possible to enter the filename given in the assessment, print a screenshot of the backup screen showing your own filename and the location of the backup data.

Task 14

Print the following reports:

- the purchases day book (supplier invoices)
- an aged trade receivables analysis
- a trial balance as at 31 October 20XX
- all sales ledger (customer) accounts, showing all transactions within each account
- the purchases ledger control account in the nominal ledger, showing all transactions within the account
- an audit trail, showing full details of all transactions, including details of receipts/payments allocated to items in customer/supplier accounts and details of items in the bank account that have been reconciled.

Note that the accounting package you are using may not use exactly the same report names as those shown above, so some alternative names are shown in brackets.

Before you finish your work use the checklist below to make sure you have printed all documents and reports as specified in the assessment.

Checklist

Documents and reports	Task	X when printed
Remittance advice	7	
Screenshot of the first recurring entry set up screen	9	
Screenshot of the second recurring entry set up screen	9	
Screenshot showing the entry of the password	13	
Screenshot showing the filename of the backup data	13	
Purchases day book (supplier invoices)	14	
Aged trade receivables analysis	14	
Trial balance as at 31 October 20XX	14	
Sales ledger (customer) accounts, showing all transactions within each account	14	
Purchases ledger control account in the nominal ledger accounts, showing all transactions within the account	14	
An audit trail, showing full details of all transactions, including details of receipts/payments allocated to items in customer/supplier accounts and details of items in the bank account that have been reconciled	14	

Practice assessment 2

Dolby Decorating

Instructions to candidates

This assessment asks you to input data into a computerised accounting package and produce documents and reports. There are 14 tasks and it is important that you attempt all tasks.

The time allowed to complete this computerised accounting assessment is **2 hours**.

Additional time up to a maximum of 1 hour may be scheduled by your tutor to allow for delays due to computer issues such as printer queues.

It is important that you print **all** reports and documents specified in the tasks so your work can be assessed. A checklist has been provided at the end of the assessment to help you check that all documents and reports have been printed.

If your computerised accounting system allows for the generation of PDFs, these can be generated instead of hard copy prints. Screenshots saved as image files are also acceptable.

Data

Dolby Decorating has been trading for one year. They have a team of three staff to offer decorating services within the local area and also sell a range of decorating supplies. The owner is **Derek Dolby** who operates as a sole trader.

The business has previously kept manual books but from **1 March 20XX**, the accounts are to be computerised.

You are employed as a bookkeeper.

You can assume that all documentation has been checked for accuracy and authorised by Derek Dolby.

Cash and credit sales are analysed in **two** ways:

- Decorating services
- Decorating supplies

Some nominal ledger accounts have already been allocated account codes. You may need to amend account names or create other account codes.

The business is registered for VAT (Standard Accounting). The rate of VAT charged on all goods and services sold by Dolby Decorating is 20%.

All expenditure should be analysed as you feel appropriate.

Before you start you should:

- Set the financial year to start on **1 March of the current year**.
- Set the software date as **31 March of the current year**.
- Set up the company details by entering the name **Dolby Decorating** and the address: **610 Wheatley Street, Moorhall, East Arnold, EF1 5KM**. In a training environment you should add your name after the business name to identify your printouts.

Task 1

(a)   From the customer record cards below, enter the information to set up customer records.

Company name: Bingham Housing	**Customer Account Code:** BIN001
Address: Unit 4 Newstead Industrial Estate Newstead Road West Arnold WF5 7HF	**Payment terms:** 30 days **Credit limit:** £23,500.00
Contact name: Sanjay Sarma **Telephone:** 0196 745240	**Email:** info@binghamhousing.co.uk **Website:** www.binghamhousing.co.uk

Company name: Limegate Decorating Stores	**Customer Account Code:** LIM001
Address: 74 Curzon Street Arnold AF8 2FW	**Payment terms:** 30 days **Credit limit:** £4,000.00
Contact name: Hannah McPhilbin **Telephone:** 0180 360214	**Email:** hannah@limegate.co.uk **Website:** www.limegate.co.uk

Company name: Town View Property Services	**Customer Account Code:** TOW001
Address: 157a Southgate Road Arnold AF5 7NV	**Payment terms:** 30 days **Credit limit:** £26,000.00
Contact name: Mary Przada **Telephone:** 0180 240240	**Email:** accounts@townviewproperties.co.uk **Website:** www.townviewproperties.co.uk

(b)   Enter the following opening balances into the customer records as at 1 March 20XX:

Bingham Housing £12,404.40

Limegate Decorating Stores £1,605.95

Town View Property Services £3,480.00

(c)   Generate a customer activity report on screen. Check it for accuracy and, if necessary, correct any errors. You do not need to print the customer activity report.

Task 2

(a)   From the supplier record cards below, enter the information to set up supplier records.

Company name: Arnold Decorating Warehouse Ltd   **Supplier Account Code:** ARN001

Address: **Payment terms:** 30 days
417 Magdala Road
Louth   **Credit limit:** £3,000.00
LE6 8AN

Contact name: Hollie Simpson   **Email:** h.simpson@arnold_decorating.co.uk

Telephone: 0131 667778   **Website:** www.arnolddecoratingwarehouse.co.uk

---

Company name: Campbell & Son Wholesale Ltd   **Supplier Account Code:** CAM001

Address: **Payment terms:** 30 days
Unit 7
317 Manvers Road   **Credit limit:** £10,000.00
Arnold
AH6 8BF

Contact name: John Campbell   **Email:** accounts@campbell.com

Telephone: 0180 200300   **Website:** www.candswholesale.com

Company name: Walker Wallpaper Supplies   **Supplier Account Code:** WAL001

Address: **Payment terms:** 30 days
680 Davies Road
Brimfield   **Credit limit:** £10,000.00
BC2 3DR

Contact name: Matt Walker   **Email:** m.walker@walkerwallpapersupplies.co.uk

Telephone: 0117 672954   **Website:** www.walkerwallpapersupplies.co.uk

---

(b)   Enter the following opening balances into the supplier records as at 1 March 20XX:

Arnold Decorating Warehouse Ltd £976.20

Campbell & Son Wholesale Ltd £4,900.50

Walker Wallpaper Supplies £7,500.60

(c)   Generate a supplier activity report on screen. Check it for accuracy and, if necessary, correct any errors. You do not need to print the supplier activity report.

Task 3

    (a)   Using the list of nominal ledger balances below, set up nominal ledger records for each account. Select, amend or create nominal ledger codes where required.

    (b)   Generate a trial balance on screen. Check it for accuracy and, if necessary, correct any errors. You do not need to print the trial balance.

List of nominal ledger accounts as at 1 March 20XX

Account name	Debit £	Credit £
Bank		3,460.00
Petty cash	200.00	
Plant and machinery	25,600.00	
Furniture	32,802.00	
Motor vehicles	26,882.08	
VAT on sales		9,800.00
VAT on purchases	5,607.00	
Sales ledger control account*	17,490.35	
Purchases ledger control account*		13,377.30
Capital		30,000.00
Sales – Decorating services		40,605.26
Sales – Decorating supplies		23,900.50
Materials purchased	6,783.62	
Water rates	105.00	
Electricity	498.14	
Premises insurance	1,508.12	
Telephone	189.55	
Wages	3,477.20	
Totals	**121,143.06**	**121,143.06**

    *   As you have already entered opening balances for customers and suppliers you may not need to enter these balances

Task 4

Enter the following sales invoices and sales credit notes into the computer.

Sales Invoice

INVOICE

Dolby Decorating

610 Wheatley Street, Moorhall, East Arnold, EF1 5KM

FAO: Mary Przada
Town View Property Services
157a Southgate Road
Arnold
AF5 7NV

invoice no   **3010**

date   **3 March 20XX**

Decorating services	£15,780.00
Decorating supplies	£2,010.00

total	**£17,790.00**
VAT @ 20%	**£3,558.00**
Total invoice	**£21,348.00**

VAT registration number 653 4510 06

Sales Invoice

INVOICE

Dolby Decorating

610 Wheatley Street, Moorhall, East Arnold, EF1 5KM

FAO: Hannah McPhilbin
Limegate Decorating Stores
74 Curzon Street
Arnold
AF8 2FW

invoice no   **3011**

date   **4 March 20XX**

Decorating services	£800.00
Decorating supplies	£607.00

total	**£1,407.00**
VAT @ 20%	**£281.40**
Total invoice	**£1,688.40**

VAT registration number 653 4510 06

Sales Invoice

```
———————————————— INVOICE ————————————————
                      𝔇olby 𝔇ecorating
              610 Wheatley Street, Moorhall, East Arnold, EF1 5KM
```

FAO: Sanjay Sarma		
Bingham Housing	invoice no	**3012**
Unit 4		
Newstead Industrial Estate	date	**20 March 20XX**
Newstead Road		
West Arnold, WF5 7HF		

Decorating services		£7,093.10
	total	**£7,093.10**
	VAT @ 20%	**£1,418.62**
VAT registration number 653 4510 06	**Total invoice**	**£8,511.72**

Sales Credit Note

```
———————————————— CREDIT NOTE ————————————————
                      𝔇olby 𝔇ecorating
              610 Wheatley Street, Moorhall, East Arnold, EF1 5KM
```

FAO: Hannah McPhilbin		
Limegate Decorating Stores	credit note no	**125**
74 Curzon Street		
Arnold	date	**5 March 20XX**
AF8 2FW		

Decorating supplies returned		£81.00
	total	**£81.00**
	VAT @ 20%	**£16.20**
VAT registration number 653 4510 06	**TOTAL**	**£97.20**

Sales Credit Note

CREDIT NOTE

Dolby Decorating

610 Wheatley Street, Moorhall, East Arnold, EF1 5KM

FAO: Mary Przada	credit note no **126**
Town View Property Services	
157a Southgate Road	date **23 March 20XX**
Arnold	
AF5 7NV	

Decorating supplies returned		£4,000.00
	total	£4,000.00
	VAT @ 20%	£800.00
VAT registration number 653 4510 06	TOTAL	£4,800.00

Task 5

Using the information from the purchases day book and purchase returns day book below, enter these transactions into the computer.

Date 20XX	Supplier	Invoice number	Gross	VAT	Net
02-Mar	Walker Wallpaper Supplies	INV 2978	1,872.00	312.00	1,560.00
05-Mar	Campbell & Son Wholesale Ltd	D03024	3,914.21	652.37	3,261.84
07-Mar	Arnold Decorating Warehouse Ltd	PI 419	1,290.96	215.16	1,075.80
	Totals		7,077.17	1,179.53	5,897.64

Date 20XX	Supplier	Credit note no	Gross	VAT	Net
14-Mar	Walker Wallpaper Supplies	CN622	134.78	22.46	112.32
18-Mar	Arnold Decorating Warehouse Ltd	87	38.02	6.34	31.68
	Totals		172.80	28.80	144.00

Task 6

Enter the following customer receipts from the documents below.

BACS REMITTANCE ADVICE

TO	FROM
Dolby Decorating	Bingham Housing
610 Wheatley Street	Unit 4, Newstead Industrial Estate
Moorhall	Newstead Road
East Arnold	West Arnold
EF1 5KM	WF5 7HF

Date 2 March 20XX

Your ref	Our ref	Amount
O/bal	PO3647	£12,404.40
	Total	**£12,404.40**

THIS HAS BEEN PAID BY BACS CREDIT TRANSFER DIRECTLY TO YOUR BANK ACCOUNT

BACS REMITTANCE ADVICE

TO	FROM
Dolby Decorating	Limegate Decorating Stores
610 Wheatley Street	74 Curzon Street
Moorhall	Arnold
East Arnold	AF8 2FW
EF1 5KM	

Date 10 March 20XX

Your ref	Our ref	Amount
INV3011	PO10345	£1,688.40
CN125	PO10247	£97.20
	Total	**£1,591.20**

THIS HAS BEEN PAID BY BACS CREDIT TRANSFER DIRECTLY TO YOUR BANK ACCOUNT

BACS REMITTANCE ADVICE

TO
Dolby Decorating
610 Wheatley Street
Moorhall
East Arnold
EF1 5KM

FROM
Limegate Decorating Stores
74 Curzon Street
Arnold
AF8 2FW

Date 24 March 20XX

Your ref	Our ref		Amount
O/bal	PO10098		£1,605.95
		Total	**£1,605.95**

THIS HAS BEEN PAID BY BACS CREDIT TRANSFER DIRECTLY TO YOUR BANK ACCOUNT

Wenlock Building Society
68 Clifton Road
Arnold, AF6 2BE

Date 27 March 20XX

NB: This cheque is a payment on account

Dolby Decorating

Five thousand pounds only

£ 5,000.00

A/c payee only

M Przada

210114   12361708   20-60-50   Town View Property Services

Task 7

(a) Enter the following payments to suppliers into the computer.

Payments to suppliers

Date (20XX)	Supplier	Type	£	Details
20 March	Arnold Decorating Warehouse Ltd	Cheque 020784	1,500.00	Payment on account
22 March	Walker Wallpaper Supplies	BACS	1,737.22	Pays invoice INV2978 less credit note CN622
23 March	Campbell & Son Wholesale Ltd	Cheque 020785	4,900.50	Pays opening balance

(b) Print a remittance advice for the payment to Arnold Decorating Warehouse Ltd and Campbell & Son Wholesale Ltd.

Task 8

(a)　You have received the following email. Enter this transaction into the computer.

Email	
To:	Bookkeeper
From:	Derek Dolby
Date:	21 March 20XX
Subject:	Drawings

Hello

Today I have withdrawn £175 cash out of the business bank account for personal use.

Please record this transaction. VAT is not applicable.

Kind regards

Derek

(b)　You have received the following email. Enter this transaction into the computer.

Email	
To:	Bookkeeper
From:	Derek Dolby
Date:	30 March 20XX
Subject:	Wages March 20XX

Hello

Today I sent the monthly wages payments of £4,980.00 by BACS.

Please record this transaction. VAT is not applicable.

Kind regards

Derek

(c)   A cheque has been received for the goods sold below. Enter the cash sales receipt into the computer

Cash sales receipt

Dolby Decorating	Receipt No: 87
	date 13 March 20XX

description	amount	
	£	p
Decorating supplies	519	00
Total (Including VAT @ 20%)	519	00

Dolby Decorating, 610 Wheatley Street, Moorhall, East Arnold, EF1 5KM
VAT reg no. 653 4510 06

Task 9

Refer to the standing order/direct debit schedule below.

(a)   Set up a recurring entry for each of the transactions below.

(b)   Print a screenshot of the screen setting up each of the recurring entries.

(c)   Process the first payment for each standing order/direct debit.

Details	Amount	Frequency	Total number of payments	Payment start date 20XX
TO: TK Telephones DD payments for telephone bill	£84.00 plus VAT	Monthly	6	18 March
TO: Moorhall Rentals STO payments for photocopier rental payments (Equipment Leasing)	£106.00 plus VAT	Quarterly	4	20 March

Task 10

(a)   A petty cash reimbursement request has been received for £50.00 to restore the petty cash account to £250.00. Enter a transfer from the bank account to the petty cash account for this amount using cheque number 020783 dated 1 March 20XX.

(b)   Enter the following petty cash vouchers into the computer.

petty cash voucher		Number *184*	
	date	*3 March 20XX*	
description		amount	
		£	p
X4 boxes of pens (VAT included)		5	60
		5	60
Receipt attached			

petty cash voucher		Number *185*	
	date	*9 March 20XX*	
description		amount	
		£	p
Cleaning materials		6	20
VAT		1	24
Total		7	44
Receipt attached			

petty cash voucher		Number *186*	
	date	*15 March 20XX*	
description		amount	
		£	p
Postage for a parcel (no VAT)		7	50
		7	50
Receipt attached			

```
┌─────────────────────────────────────────────────────────┐
│  petty cash voucher              Number  187              │
│                          date    23 March 20XX            │
│  ─────────────────────────────────────────────────────   │
│  description                               amount         │
│  ─────────────────────────────────────┬────────┬──────    │
│                                        │   £    │   p      │
│  Postage stamps (no VAT)               │   21   │  00      │
│                                        ├────────┼──────    │
│                                        │   21   │  00      │
│  Receipt attached                      │        │          │
│                                        │        │          │
└─────────────────────────────────────────────────────────┘
```

Task 11

Enter the following journal into the computer.

Journal entry 006 30 March 20XX	Dr	Cr
Sales – Decorating supplies	46.00	
Sales – Decorating services		46.00
Correction of posting error. Decorating supplies should have been posted as decorating services.		

Task 12

Refer to the following bank statement.

(a) Enter the bank charges (no VAT) and rates (no VAT) which have not yet been accounted for.

(b) Reconcile the bank statement. If the bank statement does not reconcile, check your work and make the necessary corrections.

MAIN STREET BANK PLC

Statement of account

Main Street Bank plc
25 Main Street
Arnold
AF6 8NG

Account
Dolby Decorating
610 Wheatley Street
Moorhall
East Arnold
EF1 5KM

Account number: 85426474
Sort code: 20-87-36

Date: 31 March 20XX

Date	Details	Debit £	Credit £	Balance £	
01-Mar	Opening balance			−3460.00	D
03-Mar	020783	50.00		−3510.00	D
05-Mar	BACS Bingham Housing		12404.40	8894.40	C
06-Mar	BACS Limegate		1591.20	10485.60	C
18-Mar	DD TK Telephones	100.80		10384.80	C
19-Mar	Credit 10650		519.00	10903.80	C
20-Mar	STO Moorhall Rentals	127.20		10776.60	C
21-Mar	Cash withdrawal	175.00		10601.60	C
25-Mar	BACS Walker	1737.22		8864.38	C
26-Mar	020784	1500.00		7364.38	C
26-Mar	DD Arnold City Council	130.00		7234.38	C
27-Mar	BACS Limegate		1605.95	8840.33	C
30-Mar	020785	4900.50		3939.83	C
30-Mar	BACS Wages	4980.00		−1040.17	D
31-Mar	Bank charges ✓	18.00		−1058.17	D

D = Debit   C = Credit

Task 13

(a) Use the password 'DOLd874' to protect your accounting data and print a screenshot showing the entry of the password into the computer.

If it is not possible to enter the password given in the assessment, print a screenshot showing the entry of your own password (eg at the login stage).

(b) Back up your work to a suitable storage medium using a filename made up of your name followed by DDbackup. For example if your name is Nathan Jenkin the filename would be 'NathanJenkinDDbackup'. Print a screenshot of the backup screen showing the location of the backup data.

If it is not possible to enter the filename given in the assessment, print a screenshot of the backup screen showing your own filename and the location of the backup data.

Task 14

Print the following reports:

- an aged trade payables analysis
- the purchase returns day book (supplier credit notes)
- the sales day book (customer invoices)
- a trial balance as at 31 March 20XX
- all purchase ledger (supplier) accounts, showing all transactions within each account
- the sales ledger control account in the nominal ledger accounts, showing all transactions within the account
- the sales ledger (customer) account for Bingham Housing only, showing all transactions within the account
- an audit trail, showing full details of all transactions, including details of receipts/payments allocated to items in customer/supplier accounts and details of items in the bank account that have been reconciled.

Note that the accounting package you are using may not use exactly the same report names as those shown above, so some alternative names are shown in brackets.

Before you finish your work use the checklist below to make sure you have printed all documents and reports as specified in the assessment.

Checklist

Documents and reports	Task	X when printed
Remittance advice for Arnold Decorating Warehouse Ltd	7	
Remittance advice for Campbell & Son Wholesale Ltd	7	
Screenshot of the first recurring entry set up screen	9	
Screenshot of the second recurring entry set up screen	9	
Screenshot showing the entry of the password	13	
Screenshot showing the filename of the backup data	13	
Aged trade payables analysis	14	
Purchase returns day book (supplier credit notes)	14	
Sales day book (customer invoices)	14	
Trial balance as at 31 March 20XX	14	
Purchase ledger (supplier) accounts, showing all transactions within each account	14	
Sales ledger control account in the nominal ledger accounts, showing all transactions within the account	14	
The sales ledger (customer) account for Bingham Housing only, showing all transactions within the account	14	
An audit trail, showing full details of all transactions, including details of receipts/payments allocated to items in customer/supplier accounts and details of items in the bank account that have been reconciled	14	

Practice assessment 3
Clifton Card Warehouse

Instructions to candidates

This assessment asks you to input data into a computerised accounting package and produce documents and reports. There are 14 tasks and it is important that you attempt all tasks.

The time allowed to complete this computerised accounting assessment is **2 hours**.

Additional time up to a maximum of 1 hour may be scheduled by your tutor to allow for delays due to computer issues such as printer queues.

It is important that you print **all** reports and documents specified in the tasks so your work can be assessed. A checklist has been provided at the end of the assessment to help you check that all documents and reports have been printed.

If your computerised accounting system allows for the generation of PDFs, these can be generated instead of hard copy prints. Screenshots saved as image files are also acceptable.

Data

Clifton Card Warehouse is an existing business that supplies cards, gift wrap and decorations to shops across the region. The owner is **Nathan Pearson** who operates as a sole trader.

The business has previously kept manual books but from **1 July 20XX**, the accounts are to be computerised.

You are employed as an accounts assistant.

You can assume that all documentation has been checked for accuracy and authorised by Nathan Pearson.

Cash and credit sales are analysed in **three** ways:

- Greetings cards
- Gift wrap
- Decorations

Some nominal ledger accounts have already been allocated account codes. You may need to amend account names or create other account codes.

The business is registered for VAT (Standard Accounting). The rate of VAT charged on all goods and services sold by Clifton Card Warehouse is 20%.

All expenditure should be analysed as you feel appropriate.

Before you start you should:

- Set the financial year to start on **1 July of the current year**.
- Set the software date as **31 July of the current year**.
- Set up the company details by entering the name **Clifton Card Warehouse** and the address: **340 Briarwood Road, Granby, GD7 6CA**. In a training environment you should add your name after the business name to identify your printouts.

Task 1

(a)   Set up customer records for each of the customers with opening balances as at 1 July 20XX.

Customer Account Code: AGC01 **Company name:** Ashford Gift Centre **Address:** 50 Leahurst Road, Limely Bridge, LW6 4WJ **Contact name:** Phoebe May **Telephone:** 0145 652798 **Payment terms:** 30 days **Credit limit:** £5,200.00 **Opening balance:** £4,210.32	**Customer Account Code:** BGC01 **Company name:** Brooklane Garden Centre **Address:** 125 Woodbank Lane, Limely Bridge, LK5 1VI **Contact name:** Sarah Miller **Telephone:** 0145 758201 **Payment terms:** 30 days **Credit limit:** £7,500.00 **Opening balance:** £262.50
Customer Account Code: CC01 **Company name:** Cossall Cards **Address:** 68 Granby Road, Granby, GB1 4KL **Contact name:** Agnes Nowak **Telephone:** 0152 415234 **Payment terms:** 30 days **Credit limit:** £3,000.00 **Opening balance:** £1,798.75	**Customer Account Code:** MP01 **Company name:** Michelle Proctor Ltd **Address:** 414 Cardale Road, Granby, GB7 5RD **Contact name:** Raj Singh **Telephone:** 0152 778995 **Payment terms:** 30 days **Credit limit:** £9,700.00 **Opening balance:** £3,475.20

(b)   Generate a customer activity report on screen. Check it for accuracy and, if necessary, correct any errors. You do not need to print the customer activity report.

Task 2

(a)   Set up supplier records for each of the suppliers with opening balances as at 1 July 20XX.

Supplier Account Code: BW01 **Company name:** Burton Wholesale **Address:** 57 Ged Drive, Chadderdale, CH7 4KU **Contact name:** Priya Malik **Telephone:** 0123 142124 **Payment terms:** 30 days **Credit limit:** £12,300.00 **Opening balance:** £6,203.00	**Supplier Account Code:** JFCS01 **Company name:** JF Card Supplies **Address:** 144 Standhill Parkway, Buxton Road, Chadderdale, CH2 4TF **Contact name:** Jasmin Fisher **Telephone:** 0123 872365 **Payment terms:** 30 days **Credit limit:** £7,500.00 **Opening balance:** £2,004.24
Supplier Account Code: SCS01 **Company name:** Stonebridge Card Supplies **Address:** 48 Hilton Road, Chadderdale, CH6 5YR **Contact name:** Samia Masood **Telephone:** 0123 874215 **Payment terms:** 30 days **Credit limit:** £3,000.00 **Opening balance:** £741.00	**Supplier Account Code:** WW01 **Company name:** Woolerton Warehouse **Address:** Unit 23, Colwick Parkway, Parkdale Road, Granby, GB4 9IO **Contact name:** Emilie Durand **Telephone:** 0152 748214 **Payment terms:** 30 days **Credit limit:** £11,000.00 **Opening balance:** £6,410.00

(b)   Generate a supplier activity report on screen. Check it for accuracy and, if necessary, correct any errors. You do not need to print the supplier activity report.

Task 3

(a)   Using the list of nominal ledger balances below, set up nominal ledger records for each account. Select, amend or create nominal ledger codes where required.

(b)   Generate a trial balance on screen. Check it for accuracy and, if necessary, correct any errors. You do not need to print the trial balance.

List of nominal ledger accounts as at 1 July 20XX

Account name	Debit £	Credit £
Bank	4,840.20	
Bank Deposit	6,000.00	
Petty Cash	50.00	
VAT on sales		8,780.00
VAT on purchases	1,640.00	
Furniture	34,650.00	
Capital		10,000.00
Sales ledger control account *	9,746.77	
Purchase ledger control account *		15,358.24
Sales – Greetings cards		8,741.25
Sales – Gift wrap		2,635.70
Sales – Decorations		17,636.89
Goods for resale	8,003.11	
Bank interest received		23.00
Rental income		2,100.00
Donations	345.00	
Total	65,275.08	65,275.08

*As you have already entered opening balances for customers and suppliers you may not need to enter these balances.

Task 4

Enter the following sales invoices and sales credit notes into the computer.

Sales Invoice

INVOICE

Clifton Card Warehouse

340 Briarwood Road, Granby, GD7 6CA

FAO: Phoebe May Ashford Gift Centre 50 Leahurst Road Limely Bridge LW6 4WJ	invoice no **00895** date **2 July 20XX**

Item	Quantity	Total
Rolls of wrapping paper @ 40p per roll	160	£64.00
Packs of blue balloons @ 20p per pack	250	£50.00
Packs of helium balloons @ £1.20 per pack	500	£600.00
	total	**£714.00**
	VAT @ 20%	**£142.80**
VAT registration number 542 2478 12	**Total invoice**	**£856.80**

Sales Invoice

INVOICE

Clifton Card Warehouse

340 Briarwood Road, Granby, GD7 6CA

FAO: Raj Singh Michelle Proctor Ltd 414 Cardale Road Granby GB7 5RD	invoice no **00896** date **6 July 20XX**

Item	Quantity	Total
Assorted greetings cards @ £0.62 per card	5000	£3,100.00
Banners @ £0.80 per banner	75	£60.00
	total	**£3,160.00**
	VAT @ 20%	**£632.00**
VAT registration number 542 2478 12	**Total invoice**	**£3,792.00**

Sales Invoice

INVOICE
Clifton Card Warehouse

340 Briarwood Road, Granby, GD7 6CA

FAO: Sarah Miller	invoice no	**00897**
Brooklane Garden Centre		
125 Woodbank Lane	date	**6 July 20XX**
Limely Bridge		
LK5 1VI		

Item	Quantity	Total
Candles @ £0.60 each	205	£123.00
Table decorations @ £2.50 each	110	£275.00
Assorted greetings cards @ £2.20 each	300	£660.00
	total	£1,058.00
	VAT @ 20%	£211.60
	Total invoice	**£1,269.60**

VAT registration number 542 2478 12

Sales Credit Note

CREDIT NOTE
Clifton Card Warehouse

340 Briarwood Road, Granby, GD7 6CA

FAO: Agnes Nowak	credit note no	**0074**
Cossall Cards		
68 Granby Road	date	**8 July 20XX**
Granby		
GB1 4KL		

Item	Quantity	Total
Damaged greetings cards returned @ £2.20 each	10	£22.00
	total	£22.00
	VAT @ 20%	£4.40
	Total credit note	**£26.40**

VAT registration number 542 2478 12

Task 5

Using the information from the purchases day book and purchase returns day book below, enter these transactions into the computer.

Summary of purchase invoices

Date 20XX	Supplier	Invoice number	Net	VAT	Gross
03-Jul	JF Card Supplies	INV 3079	4,271.29	854.26	5,125.55
10-Jul	Woolerton Warehouse	WW 417	2,970.05	594.01	3,564.06
12-Jul	Stonebridge Card Supplies	1784	1,333.40	266.68	1,600.08
13-Jul	Woolerton Warehouse	32546	541.30	108.26	649.56
	Total		9,116.04	1,823.21	10,939.25

Summary of purchase credit notes

Date 20XX	Supplier	Credit note number	Net	VAT	Gross
14-Jul	Stonebridge Card Supplies	CN41	174.22	34.84	209.06
16-Jul	Burton Wholesale	36	57.80	11.56	69.36
	Total		232.02	46.40	278.42

Task 6

(a)   Enter the following BACS payments received from customers into the computer.

BACS payments received listing

Date	Customer name	Amount £	Details
10 July	Michelle Proctor Ltd	3,475.20	Payment of opening balance
13 July	Cossall Cards	1,772.35	Payment of opening balance less credit note 0074 for £26.40
14 July	Ashford Gift Centre	4,210.32	Payment of opening balance
30 July	Ashford Gift Centre	1,200.00	Payment on account

(b)   Enter the following cheque received into the computer.

Cheque payments received listing

Date	Customer name	Amount £	Details
24 July	Brooklane Garden Centre	1,269.60	Invoice 00897

(c)   Print a statement of account for Michelle Proctor Ltd dated 31 July 20XX, showing all transactions that have taken place during the month.

Task 7

(a) Enter the following payments to suppliers into the computer.

Cheque stubs

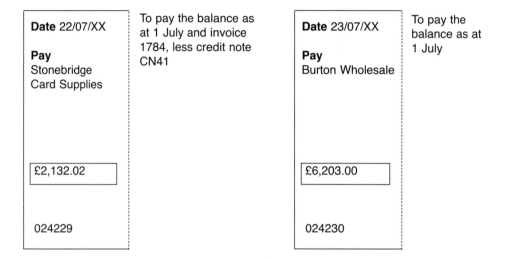

Date 22/07/XX	To pay the balance as at 1 July and invoice 1784, less credit note CN41
Pay Stonebridge Card Supplies	
£2,132.02	
024229	

Date 23/07/XX	To pay the balance as at 1 July
Pay Burton Wholesale	
£6,203.00	
024230	

Date 23/07/XX	To pay the balance as at 1 July
Pay Woolerton Warehouse	
£6,410.00	
024231	

Task 8

(a) You have received the following email. Enter this transaction into the computer.

Email	
To:	Accounts Assistant
From:	Nathan Pearson
Date:	29 July 20XX
Subject:	Transfer from deposit account

Hello

I have contacted the bank to transfer £3,000 from the deposit account into the current account.

Please record this transaction. VAT is not applicable.

Kind regards

Nathan

(b) Enter the following cash purchases into the computer.

Date 20XX	Payment method	Details	Amount
10 July	Cheque no: 024226	Farnborough Furniture – Purchase of assets – display table and shelving	£1,340.00 including VAT
14 July	Cheque no: 024227	Cromford Cards – Selection of greetings cards for resale	£299.00 including VAT
16 July	Cheque no: 024228	Full page article in the Granby News advertising Clifton Card Warehouse	£642.00 plus VAT

Task 9

(a)   You have received the following email. Set up this recurring entry into the computer but do not process the first payment.

Email	
To:	Accounts Assistant
From:	Nathan Pearson
Date:	3 July 20XX
Subject:	Recurring entry for business rates from Granby Council

Hello

I have received confirmation today that the business rates will be £123.40 per month to be taken by direct debit out of the bank account on the 15th of the month for 12 months. Please can you set up a recurring entry? VAT is not applicable.

Kind regards

Nathan

(b)   Print a screenshot of the screen setting up the recurring entry.

(c)   You have received the following email regarding an error in yesterday's email. Edit the recurring entry.

Email	
To:	Accounts Assistant
From:	Nathan Pearson
Date:	4 July 20XX
Subject:	Error in my email dated 3 July regarding recurring entry

Hello

Apologies, it would appear I emailed you the incorrect amount yesterday for the business rates direct debit. The amount should be for £132.40 per month, still to be taken on the 15th of each month but it should only be for 10 months. Please can you amend the recurring entry? VAT is not applicable.

Kind regards

Nathan

(d)   Print a screenshot of the screen showing the amended recurring entry.

(e)   Process the first payment for the direct debit.

Task 10

(a)   Enter the following petty cash vouchers into the computer.

petty cash voucher		Number 054	
		date 5 July 20XX	
description			**amount**
		£	**p**
Cleaning materials (VAT included)		12	20
		12	20
Receipt attached			
Signature *T Litchfield*			
Authorised *N Pearson*			

petty cash voucher		Number 055	
		date 6 July 20XX	
description			**amount**
		£	**p**
Donation to local charity (No VAT)		15	00
		15	00
Receipt attached			
Signature *L Moore*			
Authorised *N Pearson*			

petty cash voucher		Number 056
	date	10 July 20XX

description		amount
	£	p
Train ticket to promotional event (No VAT)	14	80
	14	80
Receipt attached		

Signature ..... *L Moore* ....

Authorised *N Pearson* ....

---

petty cash voucher		Number 057
	date	10 July 20XX

description		amount
	£	p
Pack of printer paper	5	20
VAT	1	04
	6	24
Receipt attached		

Signature ..... *T Litchfield* ....

Authorised *N Pearson* ....

(b) A petty cash reimbursement request has been received. Enter this information into the computer.

PETTY CASH REIMBURSEMENT FORM
Date: 11 July 20XX
Amount: £48.24
Cheque payable to: cash
Cheque number: 024225
Details: Restore the petty cash account
Signed: *N Pearson*

Task 11

Enter the following journal into the computer.

Journal entry 012 30 July 20XX	Dr	Cr
Office equipment	3,748.00	
Furniture		3,748.00
Correction of posting error. Office equipment incorrectly posted to the furniture account.		

Task 12

Refer to the following bank statement.

(a) On the statement below there is a BACS receipt from Ashford Gift Centre for £856.80 to pay invoice 00895, no remittance advice was received therefore the transaction has not been accounted for. Enter this transaction (no VAT) into the computer.

(b) Enter the bank charges (no VAT) which have not yet been accounted for.

(c) Reconcile the bank statement. If the bank statement does not reconcile, check your work and make the necessary corrections.

HIGHFIELD BUILDING SOCIETY

Statement of account

Highfield Building Society
126 Granby Road
Granby
GB6 8TS

Account
Clifton Card Warehouse
340 Briarwood Road
Granby
GD7 6CA

Account:	21475894
Sort code:	23-24-74
Date:	31 July 20XX

Date	Details	Debit £	Credit £	Balance £	
01-Jul	Opening balance			4840.20	C
05-Jul	BACS Ashford Gift Centre		856.80	5697.00	C
10-Jul	BACS Michelle Proctor		3475.20	9172.20	C
13-Jul	BACS Cossall Cards		1772.35	10944.55	C
14-Jul	BACS Ashford Gift Centre		4210.32	15154.87	C
15-Jul	DD Granby Council - Rates	132.40		15022.47	C
16-Jul	024225	48.24		14974.23	C
18-Jul	024226	1340.00		13634.23	C
19-Jul	024227	299.00		13335.23	C
21-Jul	024228	770.40		12564.83	C
27-Jul	024229	2132.02		10432.81	C
28-Jul	024230	6203.00		4229.81	C
29-Jul	Credit 10750		1269.60	5499.41	C
29-Jul	Transfer from 25461230		3000.00	8499.41	C
30-Jul	BACS Ashford Gift Centre		1200.00	9699.41	C
30-Jul	Bank charges	22.00		9677.41	C
	D = Debit C = Credit				

Task 13

    (a)   Use the password 'CCWIn287' to protect your accounting data and print a screenshot showing the entry of the password into the computer.

            If it is not possible to enter the password given in the assessment, print a screenshot showing the entry of your own password (eg at the login stage).

    (b)   Back up your work to a suitable storage medium using a filename made up of your name followed by CCWbackup. For example if your name is Chris Williamson the filename would be 'WilliamsonCCWbackup'. Print a screenshot of the backup screen showing the location of the backup data.

            If it is not possible to enter the filename given in the assessment, print a screenshot of the backup screen showing your own filename and the location of the backup data.

Task 14

Print the following reports:

- the sales returns day book (customer credit notes)

- an aged trade receivables analysis

- the purchases day book (supplier invoices)

- a trial balance as at 31 July 20XX

- all sales ledger (customer) accounts, showing all transactions within each account

- the bank current account in the nominal ledger accounts, showing all transactions within the account

- the purchase ledger (supplier) account for Burton Wholesale only, showing all transactions within the account

- an audit trail, showing full details of all transactions, including details of receipts/payments allocated to items in customer/supplier accounts and details of items in the bank account that have been reconciled

Note that the accounting package you are using may not use exactly the same report names as those shown above, so some alternative names are shown in brackets.

Before you finish your work use the checklist below to make sure you have printed all documents and reports as specified in the assessment.

Checklist

Documents and reports	Task	X when printed
Statement for Michelle Proctor Ltd	6	
Screenshot of the recurring entry set up screen	9	
Screenshot of the amended recurring entry set up screen	9	
Screenshot showing the entry of the password	13	
Screenshot showing the filename of the backup data	13	
Sales returns day book (customer credit notes)	14	
Aged trade receivables analysis	14	
Purchases day book (supplier invoices)	14	
Trial balance as at 31 July 20XX	14	
Sales ledger (customer) accounts, showing all transactions within each account	14	
Bank current account in the nominal ledger accounts, showing all transactions within the account	14	
The purchase ledger (supplier) account for Burton Wholesale only, showing all transactions within the account	14	
An audit trail, showing full details of all transactions, including details of receipts/payments allocated to items in customer/supplier accounts and details of items in the bank account that have been reconciled	14	

Practice assessment 4

Southglade Stationery Warehouse

Instructions to candidates

This assessment asks you to input data into a computerised accounting package and produce documents and reports. There are 14 tasks and it is important that you attempt all tasks.

The time allowed to complete this computerised accounting assessment is **2 hours**.

Additional time up to a maximum of 1 hour may be scheduled by your tutor to allow for delays due to computer issues such as printer queues.

It is important that you print **all** reports and documents specified in the tasks so your work can be assessed. A checklist has been provided at the end of the assessment to help you check that all documents and reports have been printed.

If your computerised accounting system allows for the generation of PDFs, these can be generated instead of hard copy prints. Screenshots saved as image files are also acceptable.

Data

Southglade Stationery Warehouse has been trading for two years. They have recently expanded very quickly due to two large contracts to supply stationery items to local colleges. The owner is **Tanveer Mirza** who operates as a sole trader.

The business has previously kept manual books but from **1 August 20XX**, the accounts are to be computerised.

You are employed as an Accounting Technician.

You can assume that all documentation has been checked for accuracy and authorised by Tanveer Mirza.

Cash and credit sales are analysed in **four** ways:

- Ink
- Paper
- Filing and folders
- General office supplies

Some nominal ledger accounts have already been allocated account codes. You may need to amend account names or create other account codes.

The business is registered for VAT (Standard Accounting). The rate of VAT charged on all goods and services sold by Southglade Stationery Warehouse is 20%.

All expenditure should be analysed as you feel appropriate.

Before you start you should:

- Set the financial year to start on **1 August of the current year**.
- Set the software date as **31 August of the current year**.
- Set up the company details by entering the name **Southglade Stationery Warehouse** and the address: **Unit 3, 810 Southglade Road, Newbridge, NE6 6RB**. In a training environment you should add your name after the business name to identify your printouts.

Task 1

(a)   From the customer record cards below, enter the information to set up customer records.

Customer Account Code: FC01	**Customer Account Code:** FSS02
Company name: Farnsworth College	**Company name:** Fusion Stationery Supplies
Address: 179 Farnsfield Way, Newbridge, NB4 2QP	**Address:** 94 Bracebridge Road, Filey, FL6 1BD
Contact name: David Roberts	**Contact name:** Janet Spencer
Telephone: 0198 332113	**Telephone:** 0150 963424
Payment terms: 30 days	**Payment terms:** 30 days
Credit limit: £9,000.00	**Credit limit:** £22,000.00

Customer Account Code: NLC01	**Customer Account Code:** NC02
Company name: Newbridge Learning Centre	**Company name:** Northgate College
Address: 150 Northglade Road, Newbridge, NN2 1HB	**Address:** 36 Cromford Road, Filey, FW2 3GS
Contact name: Samuel Impellizzeri	**Contact name:** Lukasz Cservenyak
Telephone: 0198 213452	**Telephone:** 0150 077360
Payment terms: 30 days	**Payment terms:** 30 days
Credit limit: £8,250.00	**Credit limit:** £12,100.00

(b)   Enter the following opening balances into the customer records as at 1 August 20XX:

Farnsworth College	£6,542.20
Fusion Stationery	£3,339.90
Newbridge Learning Centre	£2,010.20
Northgate College	£7,542.00

(c)   Generate a customer activity report on screen. Check it for accuracy and, if necessary, correct any errors. You do not need to print the customer activity report.

Task 2

(a) From the supplier record cards below, enter the information to set up supplier records.

Supplier Account Code: ROS01 **Company name:** Riverside Office Supplies Ltd **Address:** 52 Riverside Way, Filey, FG1 2NP **Contact name:** Catherine Hemmingway **Telephone:** 0150 210210 **Payment terms:** 30 days **Credit limit:** £6,400.00	**Supplier Account Code:** SS01 **Company name:** Shelford Stationery **Address:** 243 Steinbeck Street, Sneinton, SD6 7HT **Contact name:** Louise Richards **Telephone:** 0197 113679 **Payment terms:** 30 days **Credit limit:** £22,000.00
Supplier Account Code: TKAS01 **Company name:** TKA Supplies **Address:** Unit 5, Yalding Industrial Estate, Newark, NE6 4AB **Contact name:** Tamara Tomlinson **Telephone:** 0121 669774 **Payment terms:** 30 days **Credit limit:** £5,500.00	**Supplier Account Code:** WSL01 **Company name:** Wilford & Son Ltd **Address:** 7 Strelley Lane, Filey, FY1 1LP **Contact name:** Ron Wilford **Telephone:** 0150 200300 **Payment terms:** 30 days **Credit limit:** £4,200.00

(b) Enter the following opening balances into the supplier records as at 1 August 20XX:

Riverside Office Supplies Ltd	£4,350.00
Shelford Stationery	£2,230.00
TKA Supplies	£3,740.60
Wilford & Son Ltd	£1,635.55

(c) Generate a supplier activity report on screen. Check it for accuracy and, if necessary, correct any errors. You do not need to print the supplier activity report.

Task 3

(a) Using the list of nominal ledger balances below, set up nominal ledger records for each account. Select, amend or create nominal ledger codes where required.

(b) Generate a trial balance on screen. Check it for accuracy and, if necessary, correct any errors. You do not need to print the trial balance.

List of nominal ledger accounts as at 1 August 20XX

Account name	Debit £	Credit £
Bank		2,403.00
Petty cash	100.00	
Motor vehicles	8,730.50	
Office equipment	12,707.70	
Capital		10,000.00
Drawings	3,319.89	
VAT on sales		6,502.40
VAT on purchases	1,870.46	
Sales ledger control account*	19,434.30	
Purchase ledger control account*		11,956.15
Sales – Ink		5,410.20
Sales – Paper		12,023.60
Sales – Filing and folders		3,704.65
Sales – General office supplies		8,945.04
Materials purchased	9,863.30	
Telephone	208.00	
Staff salaries	3,641.00	
Vehicle insurance	652.89	
Electricity	230.00	
Vehicle fuel	187.00	
Total	**60,945.04**	**60,945.04**

*As you have already entered opening balances for customers and suppliers you may not need to enter these balances.

Task 4

Enter the following sales invoices and sales credit notes into the computer.

Sales Invoice

INVOICE
Southglade Stationery Warehouse

Unit 3, 810 Southglade Road, Newbridge, NE6 6RB

FAO: Lukasz Cservenyak **Northgate College** **36 Cromford Road** **Filey** **FW2 3GS**	invoice no **007140** date **2 August 20XX**

Item	Quantity	Total
Boxes of black pens @ £2.50 per box	150	£375.00
Packs of A4 plain copier paper @ £3.50 per pack	364	£1,274.00
A4 Lever arch folders @ £4.20 per folder	500	£2,100.00
	total	**£3,749.00**
	VAT @ 20%	**£749.80**
VAT registration number 410 8796 07	**Total invoice**	**£4,498.80**

Sales Credit Note

CREDIT NOTE
Southglade Stationery Warehouse

Unit 3, 810 Southglade Road, Newbridge, NE6 6RB

FAO: David Roberts **Farnsworth College** **179 Farnsfield Way** **Newbridge** **NB4 2QP**	credit note no **047** date **6 August 20XX**

Item	Quantity	Total
Faulty ink cartridges returned @ £14.50 per ink cartridge	12	£174.00
Damaged lever arch folders returned @ £4.20 per folder	5	£21.00
	total	**£195.00**
	VAT @ 20%	**£39.00**
VAT registration number 410 8796 07	**Total credit note**	**£234.00**

Sales Invoice

INVOICE
Southglade Stationery Warehouse

Unit 3, 810 Southglade Road, Newbridge, NE6 6RB

| FAO: Janet Spencer
Fusion Stationery Supplies
94 Bracebridge Road
Filey
FL6 1BD | invoice no | 007141 |
| | date | 14 August 20XX |

Item	Quantity	Total
Packs of A4 blue paper @ £2.99 per pack	20	£59.80
Packs of A4 green paper @ £2.99 per pack	20	£59.80
Assorted highlighter pens @ £0.60 each	350	£210.00
Ink cartridges @ £44.60 per pack	50	£2,230.00
	total	£2,559.60
	VAT @ 20%	£511.92
	Total invoice	£3,071.52

VAT registration number 410 8796 07

Sales Credit Note

CREDIT NOTE
Southglade Stationery Warehouse

Unit 3, 810 Southglade Road, Newbridge, NE6 6RB

| FAO: Lukasz Cservenyak
Northgate College
36 Cromford Road
Filey
FW2 3GS | credit note no | 048 |
| | date | 16 August 20XX |

Item	Quantity	Total
Boxes of black pens @ £2.50 per box returned	7	£17.50
Packs of A4 plain copier paper @ £3.50 per pack returned	13	£45.50
	total	£63.00
	VAT @ 20%	£12.60
	Total credit note	£75.60

VAT registration number 410 8796 07

Task 5

Enter the following purchase invoices and purchase credit note into the computer. Ensure that you read any additional notes from Tanveer regarding the invoices.

Purchase Invoice

INVOICE	**TKA Supplies**
	Unit 5, Yalding Industrial Estate, Newark, NE6 4AB
	VAT registration number 214 9784 14

Southglade Stationery Warehouse Unit 3 810 Southglade Road Newbridge NE6 6RB	invoice no	**INV635**
	date	**8 August 20XX**

X2 Computers @ £580.60 each	£1,161.20
VAT @ 20%	£232.24
Total invoice	**£1,393.44**

*Hi,
When posting this invoice please note that the computers are for use in our accounts office.
Regards
Tanveer*

Purchase Invoice

Wilford & Son Ltd	INVOICE
7 Strelley Lane, Filey, FY1 1LP	
VAT registration number 478 4398 03	

Southglade Stationery Warehouse Unit 3 810 Southglade Road Newbridge NE6 6RB	invoice no	6310
	date	**9 August 20XX**

X3 Filing cabinet locks @ £2.30 each	£6.90
X4 Promotional stands for advertising @ £87.99 each	£351.96
	£358.86
VAT @ 20%	£71.77
Total invoice	**£430.63**

*Hi,
When posting this invoice please note that these items are not for resale and therefore should not be posted to purchases. You will need to code them appropriately.
Regards, Tanveer*

Purchase Invoice

INVOICE
Shelford Stationery
243 Steinbeck Street, Sneinton, SD6 7HT

Southglade Stationery Warehouse **Unit 3** **810 Southglade Road** **Newbridge** **NE6 6RB**	invoice no **012012** date **11 August 20XX**

Goods for resale	£15,740.30
VAT @ 20%	£3,148.06
Total invoice	**£18,888.36**

VAT registration number 457 1302 80

Purchase Credit Note

CREDIT NOTE
Shelford Stationery
243 Steinbeck Street, Sneinton, SD6 7HT

Southglade Stationery Warehouse **Unit 3** **810 Southglade Road** **Newbridge** **NE6 6RB**	credit note no **124** date **15 August 20XX**

Damaged goods for resale returned	£3,541.20
VAT @ 20%	£708.24
Total credit note	**£4,249.44**

VAT registration number 457 1302 80

Task 6

(a) Enter the following cheques received into the computer.

Newbridge Building Society		Date	20 August 20XX	NB: To pay the balance as at 1 August and invoice 007140, less credit note 048

Newbridge Building Society
96 Glaisdale Road
Newbridge, NB5 3MK

Date   20 August 20XX

Pay: Southglade Stationery Warehouse

Eleven thousand, nine hundred and sixty five pounds

and twenty pence only

£ 11,965.20

L Cservenyak

Northgate College

A/c payee only

321024   65712463   30-87-74

NB: To pay the balance as at 1 August and invoice 007140, less credit note 048

Arnold Bank
14 Parkdale Road
Arnold, AJ1 4FB

Date   21 August 20XX

Pay: Southglade Stationery Warehouse

Two thousand and ten pounds and twenty

pence only

£ 2,010.20

Samuel Impellizzeri

Newbridge Learning Centre

A/c payee only

217362   58931471   32-87-96

NB: To pay the balance as at 1 August

(b) Enter the following BACS payments received from customers into the computer.

BACS payments received listing

Date 20XX	Customer name	Amount £	Details
12 August	Farnsworth College	6,308.20	Payment of opening balance less credit note number 047
12 August	Fusion Stationery Supplies	3,339.90	Payment of opening balance
18 August	Fusion Stationery Supplies	2,400.00	Payment on account

(c) Print a statement of account for Fusion Stationery Supplies dated 30 August 20XX, showing all transactions that have taken place during the month.

Task 7

(a)   Enter the following payments to suppliers into the computer.

BACS Payments to suppliers

Date 20XX	Supplier	Type	£	Details
22 August	Riverside Office Supplies Ltd	BACS	4,350.00	Payment of opening balance
22 August	Shelford Stationery	BACS	16,868.92	Pays opening balance and invoice 012012 less credit note 124
22 August	Wilford & Son Ltd	BACS	5,000.00	Payment on account

Cheque stub

Date 14/08/XX	NB: To pay the balance as at
Pay TKA Supplies	1 August and invoice INV635
£5,134.04	
201635	

(b)   Print a remittance advice for the payment to Riverside Office Supplies Ltd.

Task 8

(a)   Enter the following cash purchases into the computer.

Cash purchases listing

Date 20XX	Payment method	Details	Amount
14 August	Cheque no: 201634	Advert in Southglade Times to advertise for a new member of staff. To be coded to recruitment.	£690.00 including VAT
30 August	Cheque no: 201636	Payment to Thorpe Telephones to pay a telephone bill.	£78.00 including VAT

(b)   A cheque has been received for the goods sold below. Enter the cash sales receipt into the computer

Cash sales receipt

─────────────────── **Receipt** ───────────────────

Southglade Stationery Warehouse

Unit 3, 810 Southglade Road, Newbridge, NE6 6RB

VAT Reg no. 410 8796 07

Receipt no   **94**

date   **18 August 20XX**

	£
X200 Calculators @ £1.99 each	
Total (Including VAT)	398.00

(c)   You have received the following email. Enter this transaction into the computer.

Email	
To:	Accounting Technician
From:	Tanveer Mirza
Date:	13 August 20XX
Subject:	Bank Loan received

Hi

Today the business has received a bank loan of £20,000 into the current account.

Please record this transaction. VAT is not applicable.

Kind regards

Tanveer

(d)   You have received the following email. Enter this transaction into the computer.

Email	
To:	Accounting Technician
From:	Tanveer Mirza
Date:	27 August 20XX
Subject:	Bank transfer

Hello

I have arranged a transfer from the bank current account to the deposit account for £15,000.

Please record this transaction. VAT is not applicable.

Kind regards

Tanveer

Task 9

Refer to the email below.

(a) Set up recurring entries for the transactions.

(b) Print a screenshot of the screen setting up each of the recurring entries.

(c) Process the first payment for each standing order and direct debit.

Email

To: Accounting Technician

From: Tanveer Mirza

Date: 22 August 20XX

Subject: New direct debits and standing orders to be set up

Hello

Please can you set up a monthly direct debit for a maintenance contract for the photocopier. The payment will be to PH Photocopiers for £72.60 plus VAT per month for 10 months. This will be taken from the business bank account on the 24th of the month.

Can you also set up a standing order for rental income as we will be renting out the building next door to Harris Removals for £320.00 plus VAT per month for 6 months. This needs to be set up for the 25th of each month.

Kind regards

Tanveer

Task 10

(a)   A petty cash reimbursement request has been received. Enter this information into the computer.

PETTY CASH REIMBURSEMENT FORM
Date: 2 August 20XX
Amount: £50.00
Cheque payable to: Cash
Cheque number: 201633
Details: Restore the petty cash account
Signed: *7 Mirza*

(b)   Enter the following petty cash vouchers into the computer.

petty cash voucher		Number PC301	
	date	2 August 20XX	
description		amount	
		£	p
Stamps (No VAT)		6	36
		6	36
Receipt attached			
Signature *N Sharpe*			
Authorised *7 Mirza*			

petty cash voucher		Number PC302
	date	5 August 20XX

description	£	p
1000 plastic cups for the water machine in reception	22	10
VAT	4	42
	26	52
Receipt attached		

Signature .... *N Sharpe* ....

Authorised .. *T Mirza* ....

petty cash voucher		Number PC303
	date	8 August 20XX

description	£	p
Plants for reception (VAT included)	8	30
	8	30
Receipt attached		

Signature .. *N Sharpe* ....

Authorised .. *T Mirza* ....

Task 11

Enter the following journals into the computer.

Journal entry 017 12 August 20XX	Dr	Cr
Sales – Ink	64.80	
Sales – General office supplies		64.80
Correction of posting error. Highlighter pens should have been posted to general office supplies.		

Journal entry 018 20 August 20XX	Dr	Cr
Drawings	350.00	
Materials purchased		350.00
Items purchased by Tanveer Mirza for personal use.		

Task 12

Refer to the following bank statement.

(a) Enter the bank charges (no VAT) which have not yet been accounted for.

(b) Reconcile the bank statement. If the bank statement does not reconcile, check your work and make the necessary corrections.

ARNOLD BANK

Statement of account

Arnold Bank
14 Parkdale Road
Arnold
AJ1 4FB

Account
Southglade Stationery Warehouse
Unit 3, 810 Southglade Road
Newbridge
NE6 6RB

Account: 58946421
Sort code: 32-87-96

Date: 31 August 20XX

Date 20XX	Details	Debit £	Credit £	Balance £	
01-Aug	Opening balance			−2403.00	D
02-Aug	201633	50.00		−2453.00	D
12-Aug	BACS Farnsworth College		6308.20	3855.20	C
12-Aug	BACS Fusion Stationery		3339.90	7195.10	C
13-Aug	Loan		20000.00	27195.10	C
18-Aug	BACS Fusion Stationery		2400.00	29595.10	C
19-Aug	201634	690.00		28905.10	C
22-Aug	BACS (multiple beneficiary)	26218.92		2686.18	C
23-Aug	201635	5134.04		−2447.86	D
23-Aug	Credit 102119		398.00	−2049.86	D
24-Aug	DD PH Photocopiers	87.12		−2136.98	D
25-Aug	Credit 102120		11965.20	9828.22	C
25-Aug	SO Harris Removals		384.00	10212.22	C
26-Aug	Credit 102121		2010.20	12222.42	C
27-Aug	Transfer to 58967412	15000.00		−2777.58	D
30-Aug	Bank Charges	40.00		−2817.58	D
	D = Debit C = Credit				

Task 13

(a)   Back up your work to a suitable storage medium using a filename made up of your name
        followed by SSWbackup. For example if your name is Leila Spencer the filename would be
        'LeilaSpencerSSWbackup'. Print a screenshot of the backup screen showing the location of
        the backup data.

        *If it is not possible to enter the filename given in the assessment, print a screenshot of the
        backup screen showing your own filename and the location of the backup data.*

(b)   Use the password 'SOUg689' to protect your accounting data and print a screenshot
        showing the entry of the password into the computer.

        *If it is not possible to enter the password given in the assessment, print a screenshot
        showing the entry of your own password (eg at the login stage).*

Task 14

Print the following reports:

*   the purchase returns day book (supplier credit notes)

*   an aged trade payables analysis

*   the sales day book (customer invoices)

*   a trial balance as at 31 August 20XX

*   all sales ledger (customer) accounts, showing all transactions within each account

*   all purchase ledger (supplier) accounts, showing all transactions within each account

*   the sales – general office supplies account in the nominal ledger accounts, showing all
        transactions within the account

*   an audit trail, showing full details of all transactions, including details of receipts/payments
        allocated to items in customer/supplier accounts and details of items in the bank account that
        have been reconciled

Note that the accounting package you are using may not use exactly the same report names as
those shown above, so some alternative names are shown in brackets.

Before you finish your work use the checklist below to make sure you have printed all documents and reports as specified in the assessment.

Checklist

Documents and reports	Task	X when printed
Statement of account for Fusion Stationery Supplies	6	
Remittance advice for Riverside Office Supplies Ltd	7	
Screenshot of the first recurring entry set up screen	9	
Screenshot of the second recurring entry set up screen	9	
Screenshot showing the filename of the backup data	13	
Screenshot showing the entry of the password	13	
Purchase returns day book (supplier credit notes)	14	
Aged trade payables analysis	14	
Sales day book (customer invoices)	14	
Trial balance as at 31 August 20XX	14	
Sales ledger (customer) accounts, showing all transactions within each account	14	
Purchase ledger (supplier) accounts, showing all transactions within each account	14	
The sales – general office supplies account in the nominal ledger accounts, showing all transactions within the account	14	
An audit trail, showing full details of all transactions, including details of receipts/payments allocated to items in customer/supplier accounts and details of items in the bank account that have been reconciled	14	

Practice
assessment 1
answers

Task	Transaction Type	Account(s)		Date 20XX	Net Amount £	VAT £	Allocated against receipt/ Payment ✓	Reconciled with bank statement ✓
1	Customer O/bal	CRA001		1 Oct	4,304.40		✓	
	Customer O/bal	HOM001		1 Oct	650.50			
	Customer O/bal	SHI001		1 Oct	1,670.00		✓	
2	Supplier O/bal	CHR001		1 Oct	980.00			
	Supplier O/bal	EAS001		1 Oct	2,876.50		✓	
	Supplier O/bal	MAR001		1 Oct	940.55		✓	
3	Dr	Bank current account		1 Oct	16,000.00			✓
	Dr	Petty cash		1 Oct	160.00			
	Dr	Office equipment		1 Oct	15,400.00			
	Dr	Motor vehicles		1 Oct	32,360.00			
	Cr	VAT on sales		1 Oct	7,420.60			
	Dr	VAT on purchases		1 Oct	3,930.00			
	Cr	Capital		1 Oct	15,700.00			
	Dr	Drawings		1 Oct	2,000.00			
	Cr	Sales – Gas fires		1 Oct	35,653.37			
	Cr	Sales – Electric fires		1 Oct	16,923.44			
	Dr	Goods for resale		1 Oct	4,019.56			
	Dr	Sales ledger control *		1 Oct	6,624.90			
	Cr	Purchase ledger control *		1 Oct	4,797.05			
		*If appropriate						
4	Sales inv	SHI001	Sales – Gas fires	2 Oct	13,874.00	2,774.80		
	Sales inv	HOM001	Sales – Gas fires	10 Oct	12,908.00	2,581.60		
	Sales inv	HOM001	Sales – Electric fires	10 Oct	4,600.00	920.00		
	Sales CN	CRA001	Sales – Electric fires	12 Oct	70.00	14.00	✓	
	Sales CN	SHI001	Sales – Gas fires	14 Oct	1,620.00	324.00		
5	Purchase inv	EAS001	Goods	13 Oct	3,740.00	748.00		
	Purchase CN	EAS001	Goods	17 Oct	47.00	9.40	✓	
	Purchase inv	CHR001	Repairs	25 Oct	876.00	175.20		
6	Customer receipt	SHI001	Bank	26 Oct	1,670.00		✓	✓
	Customer receipt	CRA001	Bank	26 Oct	4,220.40		✓	✓
	Customer receipt	HOM001	Bank	28 Oct	2,000.00			
7	Supplier payment	EAS001	Bank	20 Oct	2,820.10		✓	✓
	Supplier payment	MAR001	Bank	24 Oct	940.55		✓	✓
8	Bank payment	Bank	Vehicle Insurance	16 Oct	1,490.60			✓
	Cr	Bank Current		17 Oct	10,000.00			✓
	Dr	Bank Deposit		17 Oct	10,000.00			
	Bank receipt		Sales – Gas fires	29 Oct	362.00	72.40		
	Bank receipt		Sales – Gas fires	29 Oct	724.00	144.80		
	Bank receipt		Sales – Electric fires	29 Oct	146.00	29.20		
9	Bank receipt	Bank	Rental Income – DD	1 Oct	600.00	120.00		✓
	Bank payment	Bank	General rates	5 Oct	142.00			✓
10	Cr	Bank		1 Oct	40.00			✓
	Dr	Petty cash		1 Oct	40.00			
	Cash payment	Petty cash	Postage	17 Oct	8.60			
	Cash payment	Petty cash	Stationery	18 Oct	12.00	2.40		
	Cash payment	Petty cash	Stationery	18 Oct	13.75	2.75		
11	Journal debit	Wages		30 Oct	1,000.00			
	Journal credit	Drawings		30 Oct	1,000.00			
	Journal debit	Bank		30 Oct	18.00			✓
	Journal credit	General rates		30 Oct	18.00			
12	Bank payment	Bank	Bank charges	30 Oct	23.60			✓

Task 7

East Town Electrics Remittance Advice

Frances Fireplaces
24 Steinbeck Street
Firtown
East Beeston
FW6 3RB

To	EAS001

East Town Electrics
198 Grange Avenue

Wilford

WS7 2CS

Date 20/10/2014

Cheque No 020142

REMITTANCE ADVICE

NOTE: All values are shown in Pound Sterling

Date	Ref. #	Details	Debit	Credit
01/10/2014	O/Bal	Opening Balance		£ 2,876.50
17/10/2014	CN 541	Supply of goods for resale returned	£ 56.40	

Amount Paid
£ 2,820.10

Task 9

First recurring entry

Add / Edit Recurring Entry

Recurring Entry From / To

Bank A/C To	1200	Bank Current Account
Nominal Code	4904	Rent Income

Recurring Entry Details

Transaction Type	Bank/Cash/Credit Card Receipt
Transaction Ref	STO
Transaction Details	S Shaw Rental Income
Department	0

Posting Frequency

Every	1 Month(s)	Total Required Postings	6
Start Date	01/10/2014	Finish Date	01/03/2015
Next Posting Date	01/10/2014	Suspend Posting ?	☐
Last Posted			

Posting Amounts

Net Amount	600.00	Tax Code T1 20.00	VAT 120.00

OK   Cancel

Second recurring entry

Add / Edit Recurring Entry

Recurring Entry From / To

Bank A/C From	1200	Bank Current Account
Nominal Code	7103	General Rates

Recurring Entry Details

Transaction Type	Bank/Cash/Credit Card Payment
Transaction Ref	STO
Transaction Details	Gilford council rates
Department	0

Posting Frequency

Every	1 Month(s)	Total Required Postings	12
Start Date	05/10/2014	Finish Date	05/09/2015
Next Posting Date	05/10/2014	Suspend Posting ?	☐
Last Posted			

Posting Amounts

Net Amount	142.00	Tax Code T2 0.00	VAT 0.00

OK   Cancel

Task 13

(a)

Change password

(b)

Backup

Task 14

Purchases day book (Supplier Invoices)

Date:						**Frances Fireplaces**		**Page:**	1

Day Books: Supplier Invoices (Summary)

Date From: 01/01/1980
Date To: 31/12/2019
Transaction From: 1
Transaction To: 99,999,999

Supplier From:
Supplier To: ZZZZZZZZ

Tran No.	Item	Type	Date	A/C Ref	Inv Ref	Details	Net Amount	Tax Amount	Gross Amount
4	1	PI	01/10/2014	CHR001	O/Bal	Opening Balance	980.00	0.00	980.00
5	1	PI	01/10/2014	EAS001	O/Bal	Opening Balance	2,876.50	0.00	2,876.50
6	1	PI	01/10/2014	MAR001	O/Bal	Opening Balance	940.55	0.00	940.55
34	1	PI	13/10/2014	EAS001	745226	Supply of goods for resale	3,740.00	748.00	4,488.00
36	1	PI	25/10/2014	CHR001	0014582	Repairs to showroom	876.00	175.20	1,051.20
						Totals	9,413.05	923.20	10,336.25

Aged trade receivables analysis

Date:						**Frances Fireplaces**		**Page:**	1

Aged Debtors Analysis (Summary)

Report Date: 31/10/2014
Include future transactions: No
Exclude later payments: No

Customer From:
Customer To: ZZZZZZZZ

** NOTE: All report values are shown in Base Currency, unless otherwise indicated **

A/C	Name	Credit Limit	Turnover	Balance	Future	Current	Period 1	Period 2	Period 3	Older
HOM001	Homeware Showroom	£ 25,000.00	18,158.50	19,660.10	0.00	19,009.60	650.50	0.00	0.00	0.00
SHI001	Shirley Styles	£ 28,000.00	13,924.00	14,704.80	0.00	14,704.80	0.00	0.00	0.00	0.00
	Totals:		32,082.50	34,364.90	0.00	33,714.40	650.50	0.00	0.00	0.00

Trial balance as at 31 October 20XX

Date:		Frances Fireplaces		Page: 1
Time:		Period Trial Balance		

To Period: Month 1, October 2014

N/C	Name	Debit	Credit
0030	Office Equipment	15,400.00	
0050	Motor Vehicles	32,360.00	
1100	Debtors Control Account	34,364.90	
1200	Bank Current Account	10,649.95	
1210	Bank Deposit Account	10,000.00	
1230	Petty Cash	160.50	
2100	Creditors Control Account		6,519.20
2200	Sales Tax Control Account		13,725.40
2201	Purchase Tax Control Account	4,848.95	
3000	Capital		15,700.00
3050	Drawings	1,000.00	
4000	Sales - Gas fires		61,901.37
4001	Sales - Electric fires		21,599.44
4904	Rent Income		600.00
5000	Materials Purchased	7,712.56	
7000	Gross Wages	1,000.00	
7103	General Rates	124.00	
7303	Vehicle Insurance	1,490.60	
7501	Postage and Carriage	8.60	
7502	Office Stationery	25.75	
7800	Repairs and Renewals	876.00	
7901	Bank Charges	23.60	
	Totals:	120,045.41	120,045.41

Task 14 (continued)

All sales ledger (customer) accounts

| Date: | | Frances Fireplaces | | Page: | 1 |
| Time: | | Customer Activity (Detailed) | | | |

Date From:	01/01/1980					Customer From:			
Date To:	31/10/2014					Customer To:	ZZZZZZZZ		
Transaction From:	1					N/C From:			
Transaction To:	99,999,999					N/C To:	99999999		
Inc b/fwd transaction:	No					Dept From:	0		
Exc later payment:	No					Dept To:	999		

** NOTE: All report values are shown in Base Currency, unless otherwise indicated **

A/C: CRA001   Name: Cranthorne Interiors   Contact: Habibe Mahmood   Tel: 0162 748542

No	Type	Date	Ref	N/C	Details	Dept	T/C	Value	O/S	Debit	Credit	V	B
1	SI	01/10/2014	O/Bal	9998	Opening Balance	0	T9	4,304.40		4,304.40		-	-
32	SC	12/10/2014	67	4001	Electric fires returned	0	T1	84.00			84.00	N	-
38	SR	26/10/2014	Cheque	1200	Sales Receipt	0	T9	4,220.40			4,220.40	-	R
					Totals:			0.00	0.00	4,304.40	4,304.40		

Amount Outstanding	0.00	
Amount Paid this period	4,220.40	
Credit Limit £	5,000.00	
Turnover YTD	4,234.40	

A/C: HOM001   Name: Homeware Showroom   Contact: Claire Hemmingway   Tel: 0162 147526

No	Type	Date	Ref	N/C	Details	Dept	T/C	Value	O/S	Debit	Credit	V	B
2	SI	01/10/2014	O/Bal	9998	Opening Balance	0	T9	650.50 *	650.50	650.50		-	-
30	SI	10/10/2014	281	4000	Gas fires	0	T1	15,489.60 *	15,489.60	15,489.60		N	-
31	SI	10/10/2014	281	4001	Electric fires	0	T1	5,520.00 *	5,520.00	5,520.00		N	-
39	SA	28/10/2014	Cheque	1200	Payment on Account	0	T9	2,000.00 *	-2,000.00		2,000.00	-	N
					Totals:			19,660.10	19,660.10	21,660.10	2,000.00		

Amount Outstanding	19,660.10	
Amount Paid this period	2,000.00	
Credit Limit £	25,000.00	
Turnover YTD	18,158.50	

A/C: SHI001   Name: Shirley Styles   Contact: Phillip Sandford   Tel: 0178 264240

No	Type	Date	Ref	N/C	Details	Dept	T/C	Value	O/S	Debit	Credit	V	B
3	SI	01/10/2014	O/Bal	9998	Opening Balance	0	T9	1,670.00		1,670.00		-	-
29	SI	02/10/2014	280	4000	Gas fires	0	T1	16,648.80 *	16,648.80	16,648.80		N	-
33	SC	14/10/2014	68	4000	Gas fires returned	0	T1	1,944.00 *	-1,944.00		1,944.00	N	-
37	SR	26/10/2014	BACS	1200	Sales Receipt	0	T9	1,670.00			1,670.00	-	R
					Totals:			14,704.80	14,704.80	18,318.80	3,614.00		

Amount Outstanding	14,704.80	
Amount Paid this period	1,670.00	
Credit Limit £	28,000.00	
Turnover YTD	13,924.00	

The purchases ledger control account in the nominal ledger

Date:				**Frances Fireplaces**						Page:	1	
Time:				**Nominal Activity**								
Date From:	01/01/1980							N/C From:	2100			
Date To:	31/10/2014							N/C To:	2100			
Transaction From:	1											
Transaction To:	99,999,999											

| N/C: | 2100 | | Name: | Creditors Control Account | | | | Account Balance: | | 6,519.20 CR | |

No	Type	Date	Account	Ref	Details	Dept	T/C	Value	Debit	Credit	V	B
4	PI	01/10/2014	CHR001	O/Bal	Opening Balance	0	T9	980.00		980.00	-	-
5	PI	01/10/2014	EAS001	O/Bal	Opening Balance	0	T9	2,876.50		2,876.50	-	-
6	PI	01/10/2014	MAR001	O/Bal	Opening Balance	0	T9	940.55		940.55	-	-
34	PI	13/10/2014	EAS001	745226	Supply of goods for resale	0	T1	4,488.00		4,488.00	N	-
35	PC	17/10/2014	EAS001	CN 541	Goods for resale returned	0	T1	56.40	56.40		N	-
36	PI	25/10/2014	CHR001	0014582	Repairs to showroom	0	T1	1,051.20		1,051.20	N	-
40	PP	20/10/2014	EAS001	020142	Purchase Payment	0	T9	2,820.10	2,820.10	-		R
41	PP	24/10/2014	MAR001	BACS	Purchase Payment	0	T9	940.55	940.55	-		R
							Totals:		3,817.05	10,336.25		
							History Balance:			6,519.20		

Task 14 (continued)

Audit trail, showing full details of transactions

| Date: | | | | | | | Frances Fireplaces | | | | | | Page: | 1 |

Audit Trail (Detailed)

Date From:	01/01/1980		Customer From:	
Date To:	31/12/2019		Customer To:	/////////
Transaction From:	1		Supplier From:	
Transaction To:	99,999,999		Supplier To:	/////////
Exclude Deleted Tran:	No			

No	Type	A/C	N/C	Dp	Details	Date	Ref	Net	Tax	T/C	Pd	Paid	V	B	Bank Rec. Date
1	SI	CRA001				01/10/2014	O/Bal	4,304.40	0.00		Y	4,304.40	-		
		1	9998	0	Opening Balance			4,304.40	0.00	T9		4,304.40	-		
					84.00 from SC 32	12/10/2014	67					84.00			
					4220.40 from SR 38	26/10/2014	Cheque 203654					4,220.40			
2	SI	HOM001				01/10/2014	O/Bal	650.50	0.00		N	0.00	-		
		2	9998	0	Opening Balance			650.50	0.00	T9		0.00	-		
3	SI	SHI001				01/10/2014	O/Bal	1,670.00	0.00		Y	1,670.00	-		
		3	9998	0	Opening Balance			1,670.00	0.00	T9		1,670.00	-		
					1670.00 from SR 37	26/10/2014	BACS					1,670.00			
4	PI	CHR001				01/10/2014	O/Bal	980.00	0.00		N	0.00	-		
		4	9998	0	Opening Balance			980.00	0.00	T9		0.00	-		
5	PI	EAS001				01/10/2014	O/Bal	2,876.50	0.00		Y	2,876.50	-		
		5	9998	0	Opening Balance			2,876.50	0.00	T9		2,876.50	-		
					56.40 from PC 35	17/10/2014	CN 541					56.40			
					2820.10 from PP 40	20/10/2014	020142					2,820.10			
6	PI	MAR001				01/10/2014	O/Bal	940.55	0.00		Y	940.55	-		
		6	9998	0	Opening Balance			940.55	0.00	T9		940.55	-		
					940.55 from PP 41	24/10/2014	BACS					940.55			
7	JD	1200				01/10/2014	O/Bal	16,000.00	0.00		Y	16,000.00	-		01/10/2014
		7	1200	0	Opening Balance			16,000.00	0.00	T9		16,000.00	-		
8	JC	9998				01/10/2014	O/Bal	16,000.00	0.00		Y	16,000.00	-		
		8	9998	0	Opening Balance			16,000.00	0.00	T9		16,000.00	-		
9	JD	1230				01/10/2014	O/Bal	160.00	0.00		Y	160.00	-		01/10/2014
		9	1230	0	Opening Balance			160.00	0.00	T9		160.00	-		
10	JC	9998				01/10/2014	O/Bal	160.00	0.00		Y	160.00	-		
		10	9998	0	Opening Balance			160.00	0.00	T9		160.00	-		
11	JD	0030				01/10/2014	O/Bal	15,400.00	0.00		Y	15,400.00	-		
		11	0030	0	Opening Balance			15,400.00	0.00	T9		15,400.00	-		
12	JC	9998				01/10/2014	O/Bal	15,400.00	0.00		Y	15,400.00	-		
		12	9998	0	Opening Balance			15,400.00	0.00	T9		15,400.00	-		
13	JD	0050				01/10/2014	O/Bal	32,360.00	0.00		Y	32,360.00	-		
		13	0050	0	Opening Balance			32,360.00	0.00	T9		32,360.00	-		
14	JC	9998				01/10/2014	O/Bal	32,360.00	0.00		Y	32,360.00	-		
		14	9998	0	Opening Balance			32,360.00	0.00	T9		32,360.00	-		
15	JC	2200				01/10/2014	O/Bal	7,420.60	0.00		Y	7,420.60	-		
		15	2200	0	Opening Balance			7,420.60	0.00	T9		7,420.60	-		
16	JD	9998				01/10/2014	O/Bal	7,420.60	0.00		Y	7,420.60	-		
		16	9998	0	Opening Balance			7,420.60	0.00	T9		7,420.60	-		
17	JD	2201				01/10/2014	O/Bal	3,930.00	0.00		Y	3,930.00	-		
		17	2201	0	Opening Balance			3,930.00	0.00	T9		3,930.00	-		
18	JC	9998				01/10/2014	O/Bal	3,930.00	0.00		Y	3,930.00	-		
		18	9998	0	Opening Balance			3,930.00	0.00	T9		3,930.00	-		
19	JC	3000				01/10/2014	O/Bal	15,700.00	0.00		Y	15,700.00	-		
		19	3000	0	Opening Balance			15,700.00	0.00	T9		15,700.00	-		
20	JD	9998				01/10/2014	O/Bal	15,700.00	0.00		Y	15,700.00	-		
		20	9998	0	Opening Balance			15,700.00	0.00	T9		15,700.00	-		
21	JD	3050				01/10/2014	O/Bal	2,000.00	0.00		Y	2,000.00	-		
		21	3050	0	Opening Balance			2,000.00	0.00	T9		2,000.00	-		
22	JC	9998				01/10/2014	O/Bal	2,000.00	0.00		Y	2,000.00	-		
		22	9998	0	Opening Balance			2,000.00	0.00	T9		2,000.00	-		
23	JC	4000				01/10/2014	O/Bal	35,653.37	0.00		Y	35,653.37	-		
		23	4000	0	Opening Balance			35,653.37	0.00	T9		35,653.37	-		
24	JD	9998				01/10/2014	O/Bal	35,653.37	0.00		Y	35,653.37	-		
		24	9998	0	Opening Balance			35,653.37	0.00	T9		35,653.37	-		

Date:														

Frances Fireplaces
Audit Trail (Detailed)

Page: 2

No	Type	A/C	N/C	Dp	Details	Date	Ref	Net	Tax	T/C	Pd	Paid	V B	Bank Rec. Date
25	JC	4001				01/10/2014	O/Bal	16,923.44	0.00		Y	16,923.44	-	
		25	4001	0	Opening Balance			16,923.44	0.00	T9		16,923.44	-	
26	JD	9998				01/10/2014	O/Bal	16,923.44	0.00		Y	16,923.44	-	
		26	9998	0	Opening Balance			16,923.44	0.00	T9		16,923.44	-	
27	JD	5000				01/10/2014	O/Bal	4,019.56	0.00		Y	4,019.56	-	
		27	5000	0	Opening Balance			4,019.56	0.00	T9		4,019.56	-	
28	JC	9998				01/10/2014	O/Bal	4,019.56	0.00		Y	4,019.56	-	
		28	9998	0	Opening Balance			4,019.56	0.00	T9		4,019.56	-	
29	SI	SHI001				02/10/2014	280	13,874.00	2,774.80		N	0.00	-	
		29	4000	0	Gas fires			13,874.00	2,774.80	T1		0.00	N	
30	SI	HOM001				10/10/2014	281	17,508.00	3,501.60		N	0.00	-	
		30	4000	0	Gas fires			12,908.00	2,581.60	T1		0.00	N	
		31	4001	0	Electric fires			4,600.00	920.00	T1		0.00	N	
32	SC	CRA001				12/10/2014	67	70.00	14.00		Y	84.00	-	
		32	4001	0	Electric fires returned			70.00	14.00	T1		84.00	N	
					84.00 to SI 1	12/10/2014	O/Bal					84.00		
33	SC	SHI001				14/10/2014	68	1,620.00	324.00		N	0.00	-	
		33	4000	0	Gas fires returned			1,620.00	324.00	T1		0.00	N	
34	PI	EAS001				13/10/2014	745226	3,740.00	748.00		N	0.00	-	
		34	5000	0	Supply of goods for resale			3,740.00	748.00	T1		0.00	N	
35	PC	EAS001				17/10/2014	CN 541	47.00	9.40		Y	56.40	-	
		35	5000	0	Goods for resale returned			47.00	9.40	T1		56.40	N	
					56.40 to PI 5	17/10/2014	O/Bal					56.40		
36	PI	CHR001				25/10/2014	0014582	876.00	175.20		N	0.00	-	
		36	7800	0	Repairs to showroom			876.00	175.20	T1		0.00	N	
37	SR	SHI001				26/10/2014	BACS	1,670.00	0.00		Y	1,670.00	R	31/10/2014
		37	1200	0	Sales Receipt			1,670.00	0.00	T9		1,670.00	-	
					1670.00 to SI 3	26/10/2014	O/Bal					1,670.00		
38	SR	CRA001				26/10/2014	Cheque	4,220.40	0.00		Y	4,220.40	R	31/10/2014
		38	1200	0	Sales Receipt			4,220.40	0.00	T9		4,220.40	-	
					4220.40 to SI 1	26/10/2014	O/Bal					4,220.40		
39	SA	HOM001				28/10/2014	Cheque	2,000.00	0.00		N	0.00	N	
		39	1200	0	Payment on Account			2,000.00	0.00	T9		0.00	-	
40	PP	EAS001				20/10/2014	020142	2,820.10	0.00		Y	2,820.10	R	31/10/2014
		40	1200	0	Purchase Payment			2,820.10	0.00	T9		2,820.10	-	
					2820.10 to PI 5	20/10/2014	O/Bal					2,820.10		
41	PP	MAR001				24/10/2014	BACS	940.55	0.00		Y	940.55	R	31/10/2014
		41	1200	0	Purchase Payment			940.55	0.00	T9		940.55	-	
					940.55 to PI 6	24/10/2014	O/Bal					940.55		
42	BP	1200				16/10/2014	Debit card	1,490.60	0.00		Y	1,490.60	R	31/10/2014
		42	7303	0	Vehicle Insurance			1,490.60	0.00	T2		1,490.60	N	
43	JC	1200				17/10/2014	TRANS	10,000.00	0.00		Y	10,000.00	R	31/10/2014
		43	1200	0	Bank Transfer			10,000.00	0.00	T9		10,000.00	-	
44	JD	1210				17/10/2014	TRANS	10,000.00	0.00		Y	10,000.00	N	
		44	1210	0	Bank Transfer			10,000.00	0.00	T9		10,000.00	-	
45	BR	1200				29/10/2014	56	362.00	72.40		Y	434.40	N	
		45	4000	0	x2 gas fires			362.00	72.40	T1		434.40	N	
46	BR	1200				29/10/2014	57	870.00	174.00		Y	1,044.00	N	
		46	4000	0	x4 gas fires			724.00	144.80	T1		868.80	N	
		47	4001	0	x1 electric fire			146.00	29.20	T1		175.20	N	
48	BR	1200				01/10/2014	STO	600.00	120.00		Y	720.00	R	31/10/2014
		48	4904	0	S Shaw rental income			600.00	120.00	T1		720.00	N	
49	BP	1200				05/10/2014	STO	142.00	0.00		Y	142.00	R	31/10/2014
		49	7103	0	Gilford Council - rates			142.00	0.00	T2		142.00	N	
50	JC	1200				01/10/2014	020141	40.00	0.00		Y	40.00	R	31/10/2014
		50	1200	0	Bank Transfer			40.00	0.00	T9		40.00	-	
51	JD	1230				01/10/2014	020141	40.00	0.00		Y	40.00	-	
		51	1230	0	Bank Transfer			40.00	0.00	T9		40.00	-	
52	CP	1230				17/10/2014	101	8.60	0.00		Y	8.60	-	
		52	7501	0	Postage stamps			8.60	0.00	T2		8.60	N	
53	CP	1230				18/10/2014	102	12.00	2.40		Y	14.40	-	

No	Type	A/C	N/C	Dp	Details	Date	Ref	Net	Tax	T/C	Pd	Paid	V	B	Bank Rec. Date
		53	7502	0	Envelopes			12.00	2.40	T1		14.40	N		
54	CP	1230				18/10/2014	103	13.75	2.75		Y	16.50		-	
		54	7502	0	Ink for printer			13.75	2.75	T1		16.50	N		
55	JD	7000				30/10/2014	061	1,000.00	0.00		Y	1,000.00		-	
		55	7000	0	Wages incorrectly posted to			1,000.00	0.00	T9		1,000.00	-		
56	JC	3050				30/10/2014	061	1,000.00	0.00		Y	1,000.00		-	
		56	3050	0	Wages incorrectly posted to			1,000.00	0.00	T9		1,000.00	-		
57	JD	1200				30/10/2014	062	18.00	0.00		Y	18.00		R	31/10/2014
		57	1200	0	Error in the standing order			18.00	0.00	T9		18.00	-		
58	JC	7103				30/10/2014	062	18.00	0.00		Y	18.00		-	
		58	7103	0	Error in the standing order			18.00	0.00	T9		18.00	-		
59	BP	1200				30/10/2014		23.60	0.00		Y	23.60		R	31/10/2014
		59	7901	0	Charges incurred			23.60	0.00	T2		23.60	N		

Date: **Frances Fireplaces**   Page: 3
Time: **Audit Trail (Detailed)**

Practice assessment 2 answers

Task	Transaction Type	Account(s)		Date 20XX	Net Amount £	VAT £	Allocated against receipt/ Payment ✓	Reconciled with bank statement ✓
1	Customer O/bal	BIN001		1 Mar	12,404.40		✓	
	Customer O/bal	LIM001		1 Mar	1,605.95		✓	
	Customer O/bal	TOW001		1 Mar	3,480.00			
2	Supplier O/bal	ARN001		1 Mar	976.20			
	Supplier O/bal	CAM001		1 Mar	4,900.50		✓	
	Supplier O/bal	WAL001		1 Mar	7,500.60			
3	Cr	Bank current account		1 Mar	3,460.00			✓
	Dr	Petty cash		1 Mar	200.00			
	Dr	Plant and machinery		1 Mar	25,600.00			
	Dr	Furniture		1 Mar	32,802.00			
	Dr	Motor vehicles		1 Mar	26,882.08			
	Cr	VAT on sales		1 Mar	9,800.00			
	Dr	VAT on purchases		1 Mar	5,607.00			
	Cr	Capital		1 Mar	30,000.00			
	Cr	Sales – Decorating services		1 Mar	40,605.26			
	Cr	Sales – Decorating supplies		1 Mar	23,900.50			
	Dr	Materials purchased		1 Mar	6,783.62			
	Dr	Water rates		1 Mar	105.00			
	Dr	Electricity		1 Mar	498.14			
	Dr	Premises insurance		1 Mar	1,508.12			
	Dr	Telephone		1 Mar	189.55			
	Dr	Wages		1 Mar	3,477.20			
	Dr	Sales ledger control *		1 Mar	17,490.35			
	Cr	Purchase ledger control *		1 Mar	13,377.30			
		*If appropriate						
4	Sales inv	TOW001	Sales – Decorating services	3 Mar	15,780.00	3,156.00		
			Decorating supplies		2,010.00	402.00		
	Sales inv	LIM001	Sales – Decorating services	4 Mar	800.00	160.00	✓	
			Decorating supplies		607.00	121.40	✓	
	Sales inv	BIN001	Sales – Decorating services	20 Mar	7,093.10	1,418.62		
	Sales CN	LIM001	Sales - Decorating supplies	5 Mar	81.00	16.20	✓	
	Sales CN	TOW001	Sales - Decorating supplies	23 Mar	4,000.00	800.00		
5	Purchase inv	WAL001	Purchases	2 Mar	1,560.00	312.00	✓	
	Purchase inv	CAM001	Purchases	5 Mar	3,261.84	652.37		
	Purchase inv	ARN001	Purchases	7 Mar	1,075.80	215.16		
	Purchase CN	WAL001	Purchase returns	14 Mar	112.32	22.46	✓	
	Purchase CN	ARN001	Purchase returns	18 Mar	31.68	6.34		

6	Customer receipt	BIN001	Bank	2 Mar	12,404.40		✓	✓
	Customer receipt	LIM001	Bank	10 Mar	1,591.20		✓	✓
	Customer receipt	LIM001	Bank	24 Mar	1,605.95		✓	✓
	Customer receipt	TOW001	Bank	27 Mar	5,000.00			
7	Supplier payment	ARN001	Bank	20 Mar	1,500.00			✓
	Supplier payment	WAL001	Bank	22 Mar	1,737.22		✓	✓
	Supplier payment	CAM001	Bank	23 Mar	4,900.50		✓	✓
8	Bank payment	Bank	Drawings	21 Mar	175.00			✓
	Bank payment	Bank	Wages	30 Mar	4,980.00			✓
	Bank receipt		Sales – Decorating supplies	13 Mar	432.50	86.50		✓
9	Bank payment	Bank	Telephone – DD	18 Mar	84.00	16.80		✓
	Bank payment	Bank	Equipment leasing - STO	20 Mar	106.00	21.20		✓
10	Cr	Bank		1 Mar	50.00			✓
	Dr	Petty cash		1 Mar	50.00			
	Cash payment	Petty cash	Stationery	3 Mar	4.67	0.93		
	Cash payment	Petty cash	Cleaning	9 Mar	6.20	1.24		
	Cash payment	Petty cash	Postage	15 Mar	7.50			
	Cash payment	Petty cash	Postage	23 Mar	21.00			
11	Journal debit	Sales – Decorating supplies		30 Mar	46.00			
	Journal credit	Sales – Decorating services		30 Mar	46.00			
12	Bank payment	Bank	Bank charges	31 Mar	18.00			✓
	Bank payment	Bank	General rates	26 Mar	130.00			✓

Task 7

Arnold Decorating Warehouse Ltd Remittance Advice

Dolby Decorating
610 Wheatley Street
Moorhall
East Arnold
EF1 5KM

To	ARN001

Arnold Decorating Warehouse Ltd
417 Magdala Road

Louth

LE6 8AN

Date	20/03/2014

Cheque No	020784

REMITTANCE ADVICE

NOTE: All values are shown in Pound Sterling

Date	Ref. #	Details	Debit	Credit
	020784	Payment on Account		£ 1,500.00

Amount Paid
£   1,500.00

Campbell & Son Wholesale Ltd Remittance Advice

Dolby Decorating
610 Wheatley Street
Moorhall
East Arnold
EF1 5KM

To	CAM001

Campbell & Son Wholesale Ltd
Unit 7
317 Manvers Road
Arnold

AH6 8BF

Date	23/03/2014

Cheque No	020785

REMITTANCE ADVICE

NOTE: All values are shown in Pound Sterling

Date	Ref. #	Details	Debit	Credit
01/03/2014	O/bal	Opening Balance		£ 4,900.50

Amount Paid	
£	4,900.50

Task 9

First recurring entry

Add / Edit Recurring Entry ✕

Recurring Entry From / To

Bank A/C	1200	Bank Current Account
Nominal Code	7550	Telephone and Fax

Recurring Entry Details

Transaction Type	Bank/Cash/Credit Card Payment
Transaction Ref	DD
Transaction Details	TK Telephones - Phone bill
Department	0

Posting Frequency

Every	1 Month(s)	Total Required Postings	6
Start Date	18/03/2014	Finish Date	18/08/2014
Next Posting Date	18/03/2014	Suspend Posting ?	☐
Last Posted			

Posting Amounts

Net Amount	84.00	Tax Code T1 20.00 VAT 16.80

OK   Cancel

Second recurring entry

Add / Edit Recurring Entry	✕

Recurring Entry From / To

Bank A/C	1200	▾	Bank Current Account
Nominal Code	7702	▾	Equipment Leasing

Recurring Entry Details

Transaction Type	Bank/Cash/Credit Card Payment ▾
Transaction Ref	STO
Transaction Details	Moorhall Rentals - Photocopier lease
Department	0 ▾

Posting Frequency

Every	3	Month(s) ▾	Total Required Postings 4
Start Date	20/03/2014		Finish Date 20/12/2014
Next Posting Date	20/03/2014		Suspend Posting ? ☐
Last Posted			

Posting Amounts

Net Amount	106.00	Tax Code	T1 20.00 ▾	VAT	21.20

OK Cancel

Task 13

(a) Change password

(b) Backup

Task 14

Aged trade payables analysis

Date:			Dolby Decorating						Page:	1	
Time:			**Aged Creditors Analysis (Summary)**								

Report Date:	31/03/2014							Supplier From:			
Include future transactions:	No							Supplier To:	ZZZZZZZZ		
Exclude Later Payments:	No										

** NOTE: All report values are shown in Base Currency, unless otherwise indicated **

A/C	Name		Credit Limit	Turnover	Balance	Future	Current	Period 1	Period 2	Period 3	Older
ARN001	Arnold Decorating Warehouse	£	3,000.00	2,020.32	729.14	0.00	-247.06	976.20	0.00	0.00	0.00
CAM001	Campbell & Son Wholesale Ltd	£	10,000.00	8,162.34	3,914.21	0.00	3,914.21	0.00	0.00	0.00	0.00
WAL001	Walker Wallpaper Supplies	£	10,000.00	8,948.28	7,500.60	0.00	0.00	7,500.60	0.00	0.00	0.00
		Totals:		19,130.94	12,143.95	0.00	3,667.15	8,476.80	0.00	0.00	0.00

Purchase Returns day book (supplier credit notes)

Date:		Dolby Decorating							Page:	1	
Time:		**Day Books: Supplier Credits (Detailed)**									

Date From:	01/01/1980						Supplier From:			
Date To:	31/12/2019						Supplier To:	ZZZZZZZZ		
Transaction From:	1						N/C From:			
Transaction To:	99,999,999						N/C To:	99999999		
Dept From:	0									
Dept To:	999									

Tran No.	Type	Date	A/C Ref	N/C	Inv Ref	Dept	Details	Net Amount	Tax Amount	T/C	Gross Amount V
49	PC	14/03/2014	WAL001	5000	CN622	0	Credit note	112.32	22.46	T1	134.78 N
50	PC	18/03/2014	ARN001	5000	87	0	Credit note	31.68	6.34	T1	38.02 N
							Totals	144.00	28.80		172.80

Task 14 (continued)

Sales day book (customer invoices)

Date:							Dolby Decorating					Page:	1	
Time:							Day Books: Customer Invoices (Detailed)							

Date From:	01/01/1980							Customer From:						
Date To:	31/12/2019							Customer To:	ZZZZZZZ					

Transaction From:	1							N/C From:						
Transaction To:	99,999,999							N/C To:	99999999					

Dept From:	0
Dept To:	999

Tran No.	Type	Date	A/C Ref	N/C	Inv Ref	Dept.	Details	Net Amount	Tax Amount	T/C	Gross Amount	V	B
1	SI	01/03/2014	BIN001	9998	O/Bal	0	Opening Balance	12,404.40	0.00	T9	12,404.40	-	-
2	SI	01/03/2014	LIM001	9998	O/Bal	0	Opening Balance	1,605.95	0.00	T9	1,605.95	-	-
3	SI	01/03/2014	TOW001	9998	O/Bal	0	Opening Balance	3,480.00	0.00	T9	3,480.00	-	-
39	SI	03/03/2014	TOW001	4000	3010	0	Decorating services	15,780.00	3,156.00	T1	18,936.00	N	-
40	SI	03/03/2014	TOW001	4001	3010	0	Decorating supplies	2,010.00	402.00	T1	2,412.00	N	-
41	SI	04/03/2014	LIM001	4000	3011	0	Decorating services	800.00	160.00	T1	960.00	N	-
42	SI	04/03/2014	LIM001	4001	3011	0	Decorating supplies	607.00	121.40	T1	728.40	N	-
43	SI	20/03/2014	BIN001	4000	3012	0	Decorating services	7,093.10	1,418.62	T1	8,511.72	N	-
							Totals:	43,780.45	5,258.02		49,038.47		

Trial balance as at 31 March 20XX

Date:		Dolby Decorating		Page:	1
Time:		Period Trial Balance			

To Period: Month 1, March 2014

N/C	Name	Debit	Credit
0020	Plant and Machinery	25,600.00	
0040	Furniture and Fixtures	32,802.00	
0050	Motor Vehicles	26,882.08	
1100	Debtors Control Account	23,539.72	
1200	Bank Current Account	3,941.83	
1230	Petty Cash	208.46	
2100	Creditors Control Account		12,143.95
2200	Sales Tax Control Account		14,328.32
2201	Purchase Tax Control Account	6,797.90	
3000	Capital		30,000.00
3050	Drawings	175.00	
4000	Sales - Decorating services		64,324.36
4001	Sales - Decorating supplies		22,823.00
5000	Materials Purchased	12,537.26	
7004	Wages - Regular	8,457.20	
7102	Water Rates	105.00	
7103	General Rates	130.00	
7104	Premises Insurance	1,508.12	
7200	Electricity	498.14	
7501	Postage and Carriage	28.50	
7502	Office Stationery	4.67	
7550	Telephone and Fax	273.55	
7702	Equipment Leasing	106.00	
7801	Cleaning	6.20	
7901	Bank Charges	18.00	
	Totals:	143,619.63	143,619.63

All purchase ledger (supplier) accounts

Date:					**Dolby Decorating**					Page:	1
Time:					**Supplier Activity (Detailed)**						

Date From:	01/01/1980		Supplier From:	
Date To:	31/03/2014		Supplier To:	ZZZZZZZZ
Transaction From:	1		N/C From:	
Transaction To:	99,999,999		N/C To:	99999999
Inc b/fwd transaction:	No		Dept From:	0
Exc later payment:	No		Dept To:	999

** NOTE: All report values are shown in Base Currency, unless otherwise indicated **

A/C: ARN001 **Name:** Arnold Decorating Warehouse Ltd   **Contact:** Hollie Simpson   **Tel:** 0131 667778

No	Type	Date	Ref	N/C	Details	Dept	T/C	Value	O/S	Debit	Credit	V	B
4	PI	01/03/2014	O/Bal	9998	Opening Balance	0	T9	976.20 *	976.20		976.20	-	-
48	PI	07/03/2014	PI 419	5000	Purchases	0	T1	1,290.96 *	1,290.96		1,290.96	N	-
50	PC	18/03/2014	87	5000	Purchase returns	0	T1	38.02 *	-38.02	38.02		N	-
55	PA	20/03/2014	020784	1200	Payment on Account	0	T9	1,500.00 *	-1,500.00	1,500.00		-	R
					Totals:			729.14	729.14	1,538.02	2,267.16		

Amount Outstanding	729.14
Amount paid this period	1,500.00
Credit Limit £	3,000.00
Turnover YTD	2,020.32

A/C: CAM001 **Name:** Campbell & Son Wholesale Ltd   **Contact:** John Campbell   **Tel:** 0180 200300

No	Type	Date	Ref	N/C	Details	Dept	T/C	Value	O/S	Debit	Credit	V	B
5	PI	01/03/2014	O/Bal	9998	Opening Balance	0	T9	4,900.50	0.00		4,900.50	-	-
47	PI	05/03/2014	D03024	5000	Purchases	0	T1	3,914.21 *	3,914.21		3,914.21	N	-
57	PP	23/03/2014	020785	1200	Purchase Payment	0	T9	4,900.50	0.00	4,900.50		-	R
					Totals:			3,914.21	3,914.21	4,900.50	8,814.71		

Amount Outstanding	3,914.21
Amount paid this period	4,900.50
Credit Limit £	10,000.00
Turnover YTD	8,162.34

A/C: WAL001 **Name:** Walker Wallpaper Supplies   **Contact:** Matt Walker   **Tel:** 0117 672954

No	Type	Date	Ref	N/C	Details	Dept	T/C	Value	O/S	Debit	Credit	V	B
6	PI	01/03/2014	O/Bal	9998	Opening Balance	0	T9	7,500.60 *	7,500.60		7,500.60	-	-
46	PI	02/03/2014	INV 2978	5000	Purchases	0	T1	1,872.00	0.00		1,872.00	N	-
49	PC	14/03/2014	CN622	5000	Purchase returns	0	T1	134.78	0.00	134.78		N	-
56	PP	22/03/2014	BACS	1200	Purchase Payment	0	T9	1,737.22	0.00	1,737.22		-	R
					Totals:			7,500.60	7,500.60	1,872.00	9,372.60		

Amount Outstanding	7,500.60
Amount paid this period	1,737.22
Credit Limit £	10,000.00
Turnover YTD	8,948.28

Task 14 (continued)

The sales ledger control account in the nominal ledger

Date: Time:					**Dolby Decorating** **Nominal Activity**					Page:	1

Date From:	01/01/1980		N/C From:	1100
Date To:	31/03/2014		N/C To:	1100

Transaction From:	1
Transaction To:	99,999,999

N/C:	1100	Name:	Debtors Control Account	Account Balance:	23,539.72 DR

No	Type	Date	Account	Ref	Details	Dept	T/C	Value	Debit	Credit	V	B
1	SI	01/03/2014	BIN001	O/bal	Opening Balance	0	T9	12,404.40	12,404.40		-	-
2	SI	01/03/2014	LIM001	O/bal	Opening Balance	0	T9	1,605.95	1,605.95		-	-
3	SI	01/03/2014	TOW001	O/bal	Opening Balance	0	T9	3,480.00	3,480.00		-	-
39	SI	03/03/2014	TOW001	3010	Decorating services	0	T1	18,936.00	18,936.00		N	-
40	SI	03/03/2014	TOW001	3010	Decorating supplies	0	T1	2,412.00	2,412.00		N	-
41	SI	04/03/2014	LIM001	3011	Decorating services	0	T1	960.00	960.00		N	-
42	SI	04/03/2014	LIM001	3011	Decorating supplies	0	T1	728.40	728.40		N	-
43	SI	20/03/2014	BIN001	3012	Decorating services	0	T1	8,511.72	8,511.72		N	-
44	SC	05/03/2014	LIM001	125	Decorating supplies returned	0	T1	97.20		97.20	N	-
45	SC	23/03/2014	TOW001	126	Decorating supplies returned	0	T1	4,800.00		4,800.00	N	-
51	SR	02/03/2014	BIN001	BACS	Sales Receipt	0	T9	12,404.40		12,404.40	-	R
52	SR	10/03/2014	LIM001	BACS	Sales Receipt	0	T9	1,591.20		1,591.20	-	R
53	SR	24/03/2014	LIM001	BACS	Sales Receipt	0	T9	1,605.95		1,605.95	-	R
54	SA	27/03/2014	TOW001	Cheque	Payment on Account	0	T9	5,000.00		5,000.00	-	N
					Totals:				49,038.47	25,498.75		
					History Balance:				23,539.72			

Sales ledger (customer) account for Bingham Housing Only

Date: Time:				**Dolby Decorating** **Customer Activity (Detailed)**					Page:	1

Date From:	01/01/1980		Customer From:	BIN001
Date To:	31/03/2014		Customer To:	BIN001
Transaction From:	1		N/C From:	
Transaction To:	99,999,999		N/C To:	99999999
Inc b/fwd transaction:	No		Dept From:	0
Exc later payment:	No		Dept To:	999

** NOTE: All report values are shown in Base Currency, unless otherwise indicated **

A/C:	BIN001	Name:	Bingham Housing	Contact:	Sanjay Aziz	Tel:	0196 745240

No	Type	Date	Ref	N/C	Details	Dept	T/C	Value	O/S	Debit	Credit	V	B
1	SI	01/03/2014	O/Bal	9998	Opening Balance	0	T9	12,404.40		12,404.40		-	-
43	SI	20/03/2014	3012	4000	Decorating services	0	T1	8,511.72 *	8,511.72	8,511.72		N	-
51	SR	02/03/2014	BACS	1200	Sales Receipt	0	T9	12,404.40			12,404.40	-	R
					Totals:			8,511.72	8,511.72	20,916.12	12,404.40		

Amount Outstanding	8,511.72
Amount Paid this period	12,404.40
Credit Limit £	23,500.00
Turnover YTD	19,497.50

Audit trail, showing full details of transactions

Date:					**Dolby Decorating**						Page:	1
Time:					**Audit Trail (Detailed)**							

Date From:	01/01/1980				Customer From:	
Date To:	31/12/2019				Customer To:	ZZZZZZZZ

Transaction From:	1				Supplier From:	
Transaction To:	99,999,999				Supplier To:	ZZZZZZZZ

Exclude Deleted Tran:	No

No	Type	A/C	N/C	Dp	Details	Date	Ref	Net	Tax	T/C	Pd	Paid	V B	Bank Rec. Date
1	SI	BIN001				01/03/2014	O/bal	12,404.40	0.00		Y	12,404.40	-	
		1	9998	0	Opening Balance			12,404.40	0.00	T9		12,404.40	-	
					12404.40 from SR 51	02/03/2014	BACS					12,404.40		
2	SI	LIM001				01/03/2014	O/bal	1,605.95	0.00		Y	1,605.95	-	
		2	9998	0	Opening Balance			1,605.95	0.00	T9		1,605.95	-	
					1605.95 from SR 53	24/03/2014	BACS					1,605.95		
3	SI	TOW001				01/03/2014	O/bal	3,480.00	0.00		N	0.00	-	
		3	9998	0	Opening Balance			3,480.00	0.00	T9		0.00	-	
4	PI	ARN001				01/03/2014	O/bal	976.20	0.00		N	0.00	-	
		4	9998	0	Opening Balance			976.20	0.00	T9		0.00	-	
5	PI	CAM001				01/03/2014	O/bal	4,900.50	0.00		Y	4,900.50	-	
		5	9998	0	Opening Balance			4,900.50	0.00	T9		4,900.50	-	
					4900.50 from PP 57	23/03/2014	020785					4,900.50		
6	PI	WAL001				01/03/2014	O/bal	7,500.60	0.00		N	0.00	-	
		6	9998	0	Opening Balance			7,500.60	0.00	T9		0.00	-	
7	JC	1200				01/03/2014	O/Bal	3,460.00	0.00		Y	3,460.00	-	01/03/2014
		7	1200	0	Opening Balance			3,460.00	0.00	T9		3,460.00	-	
8	JD	9998				01/03/2014	O/Bal	3,460.00	0.00		Y	3,460.00	-	
		8	9998	0	Opening Balance			3,460.00	0.00	T9		3,460.00	-	
9	JD	1230				01/03/2014	O/Bal	200.00	0.00		Y	200.00	-	01/03/2014
		9	1230	0	Opening Balance			200.00	0.00	T9		200.00	-	
10	JC	9998				01/03/2014	O/Bal	200.00	0.00		Y	200.00	-	
		10	9998	0	Opening Balance			200.00	0.00	T9		200.00	-	
11	JD	0020				01/03/2014	O/Bal	25,600.00	0.00		Y	25,600.00	-	
		11	0020	0	Opening Balance			25,600.00	0.00	T9		25,600.00	-	
12	JC	9998				01/03/2014	O/Bal	25,600.00	0.00		Y	25,600.00	-	
		12	9998	0	Opening Balance			25,600.00	0.00	T9		25,600.00	-	
13	JD	0040				01/03/2014	O/Bal	32,802.00	0.00		Y	32,802.00	-	
		13	0040	0	Opening Balance			32,802.00	0.00	T9		32,802.00	-	
14	JC	9998				01/03/2014	O/Bal	32,802.00	0.00		Y	32,802.00	-	
		14	9998	0	Opening Balance			32,802.00	0.00	T9		32,802.00	-	
15	JD	0050				01/03/2014	O/Bal	26,882.08	0.00		Y	26,882.08	-	
		15	0050	0	Opening Balance			26,882.08	0.00	T9		26,882.08	-	
16	JC	9998				01/03/2014	O/Bal	26,882.08	0.00		Y	26,882.08	-	
		16	9998	0	Opening Balance			26,882.08	0.00	T9		26,882.08	-	
17	JC	2200				01/03/2014	O/Bal	9,800.00	0.00		Y	9,800.00	-	
		17	2200	0	Opening Balance			9,800.00	0.00	T9		9,800.00	-	
18	JD	9998				01/03/2014	O/Bal	9,800.00	0.00		Y	9,800.00	-	
		18	9998	0	Opening Balance			9,800.00	0.00	T9		9,800.00	-	
19	JD	2201				01/03/2014	O/Bal	5,607.00	0.00		Y	5,607.00	-	
		19	2201	0	Opening Balance			5,607.00	0.00	T9		5,607.00	-	
20	JC	9998				01/03/2014	O/Bal	5,607.00	0.00		Y	5,607.00	-	
		20	9998	0	Opening Balance			5,607.00	0.00	T9		5,607.00	-	
21	JC	3000				01/03/2014	O/Bal	30,000.00	0.00		Y	30,000.00	-	
		21	3000	0	Opening Balance			30,000.00	0.00	T9		30,000.00	-	
22	JD	9998				01/03/2014	O/Bal	30,000.00	0.00		Y	30,000.00	-	
		22	9998	0	Opening Balance			30,000.00	0.00	T9		30,000.00	-	
23	JC	4000				01/03/2014	O/Bal	40,605.26	0.00		Y	40,605.26	-	
		23	4000	0	Opening Balance			40,605.26	0.00	T9		40,605.26	-	
24	JD	9998				01/03/2014	O/Bal	40,605.26	0.00		Y	40,605.26	-	
		24	9998	0	Opening Balance			40,605.26	0.00	T9		40,605.26	-	
25	JC	4001				01/03/2014	O/Bal	23,900.50	0.00		Y	23,900.50	-	
		25	4001	0	Opening Balance			23,900.50	0.00	T9		23,900.50	-	

No	Type	A/C	No	N/C	Dept	Details	Date	Ref	Net	Tax	T/C	Paid	Amount	R	Date
26	JD	9998					01/03/2014	O/Bal	23,900.50	0.00		Y	23,900.50	-	
			26	9998	0	Opening Balance			23,900.50	0.00	T9		23,900.50	-	
27	JD	5000					01/03/2014	O/Bal	6,783.62	0.00		Y	6,783.62	-	
			27	5000	0	Opening Balance			6,783.62	0.00	T9		6,783.62	-	
28	JC	9998					01/03/2014	O/Bal	6,783.62	0.00		Y	6,783.62	-	
			28	9998	0	Opening Balance			6,783.62	0.00	T9		6,783.62	-	
29	JD	7102					01/03/2014	O/Bal	105.00	0.00		Y	105.00	-	
			29	7102	0	Opening Balance			105.00	0.00	T9		105.00	-	
30	JC	9998					01/03/2014	O/Bal	105.00	0.00		Y	105.00	-	
			30	9998	0	Opening Balance			105.00	0.00	T9		105.00	-	
31	JD	7200					01/03/2014	O/Bal	498.14	0.00		Y	498.14	-	
			31	7200	0	Opening Balance			498.14	0.00	T9		498.14	-	
32	JC	9998					01/03/2014	O/Bal	498.14	0.00		Y	498.14	-	
			32	9998	0	Opening Balance			498.14	0.00	T9		498.14	-	
33	JD	7104					01/03/2014	O/Bal	1,508.12	0.00		Y	1,508.12	-	
			33	7104	0	Opening Balance			1,508.12	0.00	T9		1,508.12	-	
34	JC	9998					01/03/2014	O/Bal	1,508.12	0.00		Y	1,508.12	-	
			34	9998	0	Opening Balance			1,508.12	0.00	T9		1,508.12	-	
35	JD	7550					01/03/2014	O/Bal	189.55	0.00		Y	189.55	-	
			35	7550	0	Opening Balance			189.55	0.00	T9		189.55	-	
36	JC	9998					01/03/2014	O/Bal	189.55	0.00		Y	189.55	-	
			36	9998	0	Opening Balance			189.55	0.00	T9		189.55	-	
37	JD	7004					01/03/2014	O/Bal	3,477.20	0.00		Y	3,477.20	-	
			37	7004	0	Opening Balance			3,477.20	0.00	T9		3,477.20	-	
38	JC	9998					01/03/2014	O/Bal	3,477.20	0.00		Y	3,477.20	-	
			38	9998	0	Opening Balance			3,477.20	0.00	T9		3,477.20	-	
39	SI	TOW001					03/03/2014	3010	17,790.00	3,558.00		N	0.00	-	
			39	4000	0	Decorating services			15,780.00	3,156.00	T1		0.00	N	
			40	4001	0	Decorating supplies			2,010.00	402.00	T1		0.00	N	
41	SI	LIM001					04/03/2014	3011	1,407.00	281.40		Y	1,688.40	-	
			41	4000	0	Decorating services			800.00	160.00	T1		960.00	N	
						97.20 from SC 44	05/03/2014	125					97.20		
						862.80 from SR 52	10/03/2014	BACS					862.80		
			42	4001	0	Decorating supplies			607.00	121.40	T1		728.40	-	
						728.40 from SR 52	10/03/2014	BACS					728.40		
43	SI	BIN001					20/03/2014	3012	7,093.10	1,418.62		N	0.00	-	
			43	4000	0	Decorating services			7,093.10	1,418.62	T1		0.00	N	
44	SC	LIM001					05/03/2014	125	81.00	16.20		Y	97.20	-	
			44	4001	0	Decorating supplies returned			81.00	16.20	T1		97.20	N	
						97.20 to SI 41	05/03/2014	3011					97.20		
45	SC	TOW001					23/03/2014	126	4,000.00	800.00		N	0.00	-	
			45	4001	0	Decorating supplies returned			4,000.00	800.00	T1		0.00	N	
46	PI	WAL001					02/03/2014	INV 2978	1,560.00	312.00		Y	1,872.00	-	
			46	5000	0	Purchases			1,560.00	312.00	T1		1,872.00	N	
						134.78 from PC 49	14/03/2014	CN622					134.78		
						1737.22 from PP 56	22/03/2014	BACS					1,737.22		
47	PI	CAM001					05/03/2014	D03024	3,261.84	652.37		N	0.00	-	
			47	5000	0	Purchases			3,261.84	652.37	T1		0.00	N	
48	PI	ARN001					07/03/2014	PI 419	1,075.80	215.16		N	0.00	-	
			48	5000	0	Purchases			1,075.80	215.16	T1		0.00	N	
49	PC	WAL001					14/03/2014	CN622	112.32	22.46		Y	134.78	-	
			49	5000	0	Credit note			112.32	22.46	T1		134.78	N	
						134.78 to PI 46	14/03/2014	INV 2978					134.78		
50	PC	ARN001					18/03/2014	87	31.68	6.34		N	0.00	-	
			50	5000	0	Credit note			31.68	6.34	T1		0.00	N	
51	SR	BIN001					02/03/2014	BACS	12,404.40	0.00		Y	12,404.40	R	31/03/2014
			51	1200	0	Sales Receipt			12,404.40	0.00	T9		12,404.40	-	
						12404.40 to SI 1	02/03/2014	O/bal					12,404.40		
52	SR	LIM001					10/03/2014	BACS	1,591.20	0.00		Y	1,591.20	R	31/03/2014
			52	1200	0	Sales Receipt			1,591.20	0.00	T9		1,591.20	-	
						862.80 to SI 41	10/03/2014	3011					862.80		
						728.40 to SI 42	10/03/2014	3011					728.40		
53	SR	LIM001					24/03/2014	BACS	1,605.95	0.00		Y	1,605.95	R	31/03/2014
			53	1200	0	Sales Receipt			1,605.95	0.00	T9		1,605.95	-	
						1605.95 to SI 2	24/03/2014	O/bal					1,605.95		
54	SA	TOW001					27/03/2014	Cheque	5,000.00	0.00		N	0.00	N	
			54	1200	0	Payment on Account			5,000.00	0.00	T9		0.00	-	
55	PA	ARN001					20/03/2014	020784	1,500.00	0.00		N	0.00	R	31/03/2014
			55	1200	0	Payment on Account			1,500.00	0.00	T9		0.00	-	

No	Type	A/C / N/C	Dept	Details	Date	Ref	Net	Tax	T/C	Paid	Amount	B	Date
56	PP	WAL001			22/03/2014	BACS	1,737.22	0.00		Y	1,737.22	R	31/03/2014
		56 / 1200	0	Purchase Payment			1,737.22	0.00	T9		1,737.22	-	
				1737.22 to PI 46	22/03/2014	INV 2978					1,737.22		
57	PP	CAM001			23/03/2014	020785	4,900.50	0.00		Y	4,900.50	R	31/03/2014
		57 / 1200	0	Purchase Payment			4,900.50	0.00	T9		4,900.50	-	
				4900.50 to PI 5	23/03/2014	O/bal					4,900.50		
58	BP	1200			21/03/2014	Cash	175.00	0.00		Y	175.00	R	31/03/2014
		58 / 3050	0	Cash withdrawn for personal use			175.00	0.00	T9		175.00	-	
59	BP	1200			30/03/2014	BACS	4,980.00	0.00		Y	4,980.00	R	31/03/2014
		59 / 7004	0	Monthly wages			4,980.00	0.00	T9		4,980.00	-	
60	BR	1200			13/03/2014	87	432.50	86.50		Y	519.00	R	31/03/2014
		60 / 4001	0	Decorating supplies - cash sale			432.50	86.50	T1		519.00	N	
61	BP	1200			18/03/2014	DD	84.00	16.80		Y	100.80	R	31/03/2014
		61 / 7550	0	TK Telephones			84.00	16.80	T1		100.80	N	
62	BP	1200			20/03/2014	STO	106.00	21.20		Y	127.20	R	31/03/2014
		62 / 7702	0	Moorhall Rentals - Photocopier			106.00	21.20	T1		127.20	N	
63	JC	1200			01/03/2014	020783	50.00	0.00		Y	50.00	R	31/03/2014
		63 / 1200	0	Bank Transfer - Restore petty cash			50.00	0.00	T9		50.00	-	
64	JD	1230			01/03/2014	020783	50.00	0.00		Y	50.00	-	
		64 / 1230	0	Bank Transfer - Restore petty cash			50.00	0.00	T9		50.00	-	
65	CP	1230			03/03/2014	184	4.67	0.93		Y	5.60	-	
		65 / 7502	0	x4 boxes of pens			4.67	0.93	T1		5.60	N	
66	CP	1230			09/03/2014	185	6.20	1.24		Y	7.44	-	
		66 / 7801	0	Cleaning materials			6.20	1.24	T1		7.44	N	
67	CP	1230			15/03/2014	186	7.50	0.00		Y	7.50	-	
		67 / 7501	0	Parcel			7.50	0.00	T2		7.50	N	
68	CP	1230			23/03/2014	187	21.00	0.00		Y	21.00	-	
		68 / 7501	0	Postage stamps			21.00	0.00	T2		21.00	N	
69	JD	4001			30/03/2014	006	46.00	0.00		Y	46.00	-	
		69 / 4001	0	Correction of error			46.00	0.00	T9		46.00	-	
70	JC	4000			30/03/2014	006	46.00	0.00		Y	46.00	-	
		70 / 4000	0	Correction of error			46.00	0.00	T9		46.00	-	
71	BP	1200			31/03/2014	DD	18.00	0.00		Y	18.00	R	31/03/2014
		71 / 7901	0	Bank charges			18.00	0.00	T2		18.00	N	
72	BP	1200			26/03/2014	DD	130.00	0.00		Y	130.00	R	31/03/2014
		72 / 7103	0	Arnold City Council			130.00	0.00	T2		130.00	N	

Practice assessment 3 answers

Task	Transaction Type	Account(s)		Date 20XX	Net Amount £	VAT £	Allocated against receipt/ Payment ✓	Reconciled with bank statement ✓
1	Customer O/bal	AGC01		1 July	4,210.32		✓	
	Customer O/bal	BGC01		1 July	262.50			
	Customer O/bal	CC01		1 July	1,798.75		✓	
	Customer O/bal	MP01		1 July	3,475.20		✓	
2	Supplier O/bal	BW01		1 July	6,203.00		✓	
	Supplier O/bal	JFCS01		1 July	2,004.24			
	Supplier O/bal	SCS01		1 July	741.00		✓	
	Supplier O/bal	WW01		1 July	6,410.00		✓	
3	Dr	Bank current account		1 July	4,840.20			✓
	Dr	Bank deposit account		1 July	6,000.00			
	Dr	Petty cash		1 July	50.00			
	Cr	VAT on sales		1 July	8,780.00			
	Dr	VAT on purchases		1 July	1,640.00			
	Dr	Furniture		1 July	34,650.00			
	Cr	Capital		1 July	10,000.00			
	Dr	Sales ledger control *		1 July	9,746.77			
	Cr	Purchase ledger control *		1 July	15,358.24			
	Cr	Sales – Greetings card		1 July	8,741.25			
	Cr	Sales – Gift wrap		1 July	2,635.70			
	Cr	Sales – Decorations		1 July	17,636.89			
	Dr	Goods for resale		1 July	8,003.11			
	Cr	Bank interest received		1 July	23.00			
	Cr	Rental income		1 July	2,100.00			
	Dr	Donations *If appropriate		1 July	345.00			
4	Sales inv	AGC01	Sales:	2 July				
			Gift wrap		64.00	12.80	✓	
			Decorations		50.00	10.00	✓	
			Decoration		600.00	120.00	✓	
	Sales inv	MP01	Sales:	6 July				
			Greetings cards		3,100.00	620.00		
			Decorations		60.00	12.00		
	Sales inv	BGC01	Sales:	6 July				
			Decorations		123.00	24.60	✓	
			Decorations		275.00	55.00	✓	
			Greetings cards		660.00	132.00	✓	
	Sales CN	CC01	Sales: Greetings cards	8 July	22.00	4.40	✓	
5	Purchase inv	JFCS01	Purchases	3 July	4,271.29	854.26		
	Purchase inv	WW01	Purchases	10 July	2,970.05	594.01		
	Purchase inv	SCS01	Purchases	12 July	1,333.40	266.68	✓	
	Purchase inv	WW01	Purchases	13 July	541.30	108.26		
	Purchase CN	SCS01	Purchase returns	14 July	174.22	34.84	✓	
	Purchase CN	BW01	Purchase returns	16 July	57.80	11.56		
6	Customer receipt	MP01	Bank	10 July	3,475.20		✓	✓
	Customer receipt	CC01	Bank	13 July	1,772.35		✓	✓
	Customer receipt	AGC01	Bank	14 July	4,210.32		✓	✓
	Customer receipt	AGC01	Bank	30 July	1,200.00			✓
	Customer receipt	BGC01	Bank	24 July	1,269.60		✓	✓
7	Supplier payment	SCS01	Bank	22 July	2,132.02		✓	✓
	Supplier payment	BW01	Bank	23 July	6,203.00		✓	✓
	Supplier payment	WW01	Bank	23 July	6,410.00		✓	

8	Cr	Bank - Deposit		29 July	3,000.00				
	Dr	Bank - Current		29 July	3,000.00				✓
	Bank payment	Bank	Furniture	10 July	1,116.67	223.33			✓
	Bank payment	Bank	Purchases	14 July	249.17	49.83			✓
	Bank payment	Bank	Advertising	16 July	642.00	128.40			✓
9	Bank payment	Bank	General rates – DD	15 July	132.40				✓
10	Cash payment	Petty cash	Cleaning	5 July	10.17	2.03			
	Cash payment	Petty cash	Donation	6 July	15.00				
	Cash payment	Petty cash	Travel	10 July	14.80				
	Cash payment	Petty cash	Office stationery	10 July	5.20	1.04			
	Cr	Bank		11 July	48.24				✓
	Dr	Petty cash		11 July	48.24				
11	Journal debit	Office equipment		30 July	3,748.00				
	Journal credit	Furniture		30 July	3,478.00				
12	Supplier payment	AGC01	Bank	5 July	856.80			✓	✓
	Bank payment	Bank	Bank charges	30 July	22.00				✓

Task 6

Michelle Proctor Ltd Statement of account

Clifton Card Warehouse
340 Briarwood Road
Granby
GD7 6CA

MP01

Michelle Proctor Ltd   31/07/2014
414 Cardale Road

Granby

GB7 5RD

All values are shown in Pound Sterling

01/07/2014	O/Bal	Goods/Services	£	3,475.20			£	3,475.20
06/07/2014	00896	Goods/Services	£	3,792.00			£	7,267.20
10/07/2014	BACS	Payment			£	3,475.20	£	3,792.00

£	3,792.00	£	0.00	£	0.00	£	0.00	£	0.00	**£**	**3,792.00**

Task 9(b)

Recurring entry

Add / Edit Recurring Entry ✕

Recurring Entry From / To

Bank A/C	1200	Bank Current Account
Nominal Code	7103	General Rates

Recurring Entry Details

Transaction Type	Bank/Cash/Credit Card Payment
Transaction Ref	DD
Transaction Details	Granby Council business rates
Department	0

Posting Frequency

Every	1 Month(s)	Total Required Postings	12
Start Date	15/07/2014	Finish Date	15/06/2015
Next Posting Date	15/07/2014	Suspend Posting ?	☐
Last Posted			

Posting Amounts

Net Amount	123.40	Tax Code	T2 0.00	VAT 0.00

OK   Cancel

Task 9(d)

Amended recurring entry

Add / Edit Recurring Entry	✕

Recurring Entry From / To

Bank A/C From	1200 ▽	Bank Current Account
Nominal Code	7103 ▽	General Rates

Recurring Entry Details

Transaction Type	Bank/Cash/Credit Card Payment ▽
Transaction Ref	DD
Transaction Details	Granby Council business rates
Department	0 ▽

Posting Frequency

Every	1 Month(s) ▽	Total Required Postings	10
Start Date	15/07/2014	Finish Date	15/04/2015
Next Posting Date	15/07/2014	Suspend Posting ?	☐
Last Posted			

Posting Amounts

Net Amount	132.40	Tax Code T2 0.00 ▽	VAT 0.00

OK	Cancel

Task 13

(a)

Change password

Change Password	✕
Logon Name	MANAGER
New Password	✕✕✕✕✕✕✕✕
Confirm New Password	✕✕✕✕✕✕✕✕
	Discard OK Cancel

(b)

Backup

Backup ✕

Backup Company | Advanced Options | Previous Backups

Company Details

You are about to create a backup of:

Company Name: Clifton Card Warehouse

Found In: C:\PROGRAMDATA\SAGE\ACCOUNTS\2012\COMPANY.000\

Where do you want the company backed up to?

Please click Browse to select a location to save this backup to. We have suggested a filename for this backup. If you are happy with this suggestion, click OK to save the backup.

Backing Up to removable media? Insert the device before clicking OK.

Backing Up to CD? Refer to the Help now.

Filename : CCWbackup

Location : F:\

Browse...

OK   Cancel   Help

Task 14

Sales returns day book (Customer credit notes)

Date: Time:				**Clifton Card Warehouse** **Day Books: Customer Credits (Summary)**					Page:	l

Date From: 01/01/1980
Date To: 31/12/2019

Transaction From: 1
Transaction To: 99,999,999

Customer From:
Customer To: ZZZZZZZZ

Tran No.	Items	Tp	Date	A/C Ref	Inv Ref	Details	Net Amount	Tax Amount	Gross Amount
45	1	SC	08/07/2014	CC01	0074	x10 Damaged greetings cards returned	22.00	4.40	26.40
						Totals:	22.00	4.40	26.40

Aged trade receivables analysis

Date: Time:		**Clifton Card Warehouse** **Aged Debtors Analysis (Summary)**							Page:	l

Report Date: 31/07/2014
Include future transactions: No
Exclude later payments: No

Customer From:
Customer To: ZZZZZZZZ

** NOTE: All report values are shown in Base Currency, unless otherwise indicated **

A/C	Name		Credit Limit	Turnover	Balance	Future	Current	Period 1	Period 2	Period 3	Older
AGC01	Ashford Gift Centre	£	5,200.00	4,924.32	-1,200.00	0.00	-1,200.00	0.00	0.00	0.00	0.00
BGC01	Brooklane Garden Centre	£	7,500.00	1,320.50	262.50	0.00	0.00	262.50	0.00	0.00	0.00
MP01	Michelle Proctor Ltd	£	9,700.00	6,635.20	3,792.00	0.00	3,792.00	0.00	0.00	0.00	0.00
	Totals:			12,880.02	2,854.50	0.00	2,592.00	262.50	0.00	0.00	0.00

Purchases day book (Supplier invoices)

Date: Time:				**Clifton Card Warehouse** **Day Books: Supplier Invoices (Summary)**					Page:	l

Date From: 01/01/1980
Date To: 31/12/2019

Transaction From: 1
Transaction To: 99,999,999

Supplier From:
Supplier To: ZZZZZZZZ

Tran No.	Item	Type	Date	A/C Ref	Inv Ref	Details	Net Amount	Tax Amount	Gross Amount
5	1	PI	01/07/2014	BW01	O/Bal	Opening Balance	6,203.00	0.00	6,203.00
6	1	PI	01/07/2014	JFCS01	O/Bal	Opening Balance	2,004.24	0.00	2,004.24
7	1	PI	01/07/2014	SCS01	O/Bal	Opening Balance	741.00	0.00	741.00
8	1	PI	01/07/2014	WW01	O/Bal	Opening Balance	6,410.00	0.00	6,410.00
46	1	PI	03/07/2014	JFCS01	INV 3079	Purchases	4,271.29	854.26	5,125.55
47	1	PI	10/07/2014	WW01	WW 417	Purchases	2,970.05	594.01	3,564.06
48	1	PI	12/07/2014	SCS01	1784	Purchases	1,333.40	266.68	1,600.08
49	1	PI	13/07/2014	WW01	32546	Purchases	541.30	108.26	649.56
						Totals	24,474.28	1,823.21	26,297.49

Trial balance as at 31 July 20XX

Date:		Clifton Card Warehouse	Page: 1
Time:		Period Trial Balance	

To Period: Month 1, July 2014

N/C	Name	Debit	Credit
0030	Office Equipment	3,748.00	
0040	Furniture and Fixtures	32,018.67	
1100	Debtors Control Account	2,854.50	
1200	Bank Current Account	3,267.41	
1210	Bank Deposit Account	3,000.00	
1230	Petty Cash	50.00	
2100	Creditors Control Account		11,274.05
2200	Sales Tax Control Account		9,762.00
2201	Purchase Tax Control Account	3,821.44	
3000	Capital		10,000.00
4000	Sales - Greetings Cards		12,479.25
4001	Sales - Gift Wrap		2,699.70
4002	Sales - Decorations		18,744.89
4904	Rent Income		2,100.00
4906	Bank Interest Received		23.00
5000	Materials Purchased	17,136.30	
6201	Advertising	642.00	
7103	General Rates	132.40	
7400	Travelling	14.80	
7502	Office Stationery	5.20	
7801	Cleaning	10.17	
7901	Bank Charges	22.00	
8200	Donations	360.00	
	Totals:	67,082.89	67,082.89

Task 14 (continued)

All sales ledger (customer) accounts

Date:				**Clifton Card Warehouse**					Page:	1
Time:				**Customer Activity (Detailed)**						

Date From:	01/01/1980					Customer From:			
Date To:	31/07/2014					Customer To:	*ZZZZZZZZ*		
Transaction From:	1					N/C From:			
Transaction To:	99,999,999					N/C To:	99999999		
Inc b/fwd transaction:	No					Dept From:	0		
Exc later payment:	No					Dept To:	999		

** NOTE: All report values are shown in Base Currency, unless otherwise indicated **

A/C: AGC01   Name: Ashford Gift Centre   Contact: Phoebe May   Tel: 0145 652798

No	Type	Date	Ref	N/C	Details	Dept	T/C	Value	O/S	Debit	Credit	V	B
1	SI	01/07/2014	O/Bal	9998	Opening Balance	0	T9	4,210.32		4,210.32		-	-
37	SI	02/07/2014	00895	4001	x160 Rolls of wrapping paper	0	T1	76.80		76.80		N	-
38	SI	02/07/2014	00895	4002	x250 Packs of blue balloons	0	T1	60.00		60.00		N	-
39	SI	02/07/2014	00895	4002	x500 Packs of helium balloons	0	T1	720.00		720.00		N	-
54	SR	14/07/2014	BACS	1200	Sales Receipt	0	T9	4,210.32			4,210.32	-	R
55	SA	30/07/2014	BACS	1200	Payment on Account	0	T9	1,200.00 *	-1,200.00		1,200.00	-	R
74	SR	05/07/2014	BACS	1200	Sales Receipt	0	T9	856.80			856.80	-	R
					Totals:			-1,200.00	-1,200.00	5,067.12	6,267.12		

Amount Outstanding	-1,200.00
Amount Paid this period	6,267.12
Credit Limit £	5,200.00
Turnover YTD	4,924.32

A/C: BGC01   Name: Brooklane Garden Centre   Contact: Sarah Miller   Tel: 0145 758201

No	Type	Date	Ref	N/C	Details	Dept	T/C	Value	O/S	Debit	Credit	V	B
2	SI	01/07/2014	O/Bal	9998	Opening Balance	0	T9	262.50 *	262.50	262.50		-	-
42	SI	06/07/2014	00897	4002	x205 Candles	0	T1	147.60		147.60		N	-
43	SI	06/07/2014	00897	4002	x110 Table decorations	0	T1	330.00		330.00		N	-
44	SI	06/07/2014	00897	4000	x300 Assorted greetings cards	0	T1	792.00		792.00		N	-
56	SR	24/07/2014	Cheque	1200	Sales Receipt	0	T9	1,269.60			1,269.60	-	R
					Totals:			262.50	262.50	1,532.10	1,269.60		

Amount Outstanding	262.50
Amount Paid this period	1,269.60
Credit Limit £	7,500.00
Turnover YTD	1,320.50

A/C: CC01   Name: Cossall Cards   Contact: Agnes Nowak   Tel: 0152 415234

No	Type	Date	Ref	N/C	Details	Dept	T/C	Value	O/S	Debit	Credit	V	B
3	SI	01/07/2014	O/Bal	9998	Opening Balance	0	T9	1,798.75		1,798.75		-	-
45	SC	08/07/2014	0074	4000	x10 Damaged greetings cards	0	T1	26.40			26.40	N	-
53	SR	13/07/2014	BACS	1200	Sales Receipt	0	T9	1,772.35			1,772.35	-	R
					Totals:			0.00	0.00	1,798.75	1,798.75		

Amount Outstanding	0.00
Amount Paid this period	1,772.35
Credit Limit £	3,000.00
Turnover YTD	1,776.75

A/C: MP01   Name: Michelle Proctor Ltd   Contact: Raj Singh   Tel: 0152 778995

No	Type	Date	Ref	N/C	Details	Dept	T/C	Value	O/S	Debit	Credit	V	B
4	SI	01/07/2014	O/Bal	9998	Opening Balance	0	T9	3,475.20		3,475.20		-	-
40	SI	06/07/2014	00896	4000	x5000 Assorted greetings cards	0	T1	3,720.00 *	3,720.00	3,720.00		N	-
41	SI	06/07/2014	00896	4002	x75 Banners	0	T1	72.00 *	72.00	72.00		N	-
52	SR	10/07/2014	BACS	1200	Sales Receipt	0	T9	3,475.20			3,475.20	-	R
					Totals:			3,792.00	3,792.00	7,267.20	3,475.20		

Amount Outstanding	3,792.00
Amount Paid this period	3,475.20
Credit Limit £	9,700.00
Turnover YTD	6,635.20

The bank current account in the nominal ledger

Date: Time:				**Clifton Card Warehouse** **Nominal Activity**						Page:	1	
Date From: Date To:		01/01/1980 31/07/2014						N/C From: N/C To:		1200 1200		
Transaction From: Transaction To:		1 99,999,999										

N/C:	1200		Name:	Bank Current Account				Account Balance:		3,267.41 DR		

No	Type	Date	Account	Ref	Details	Dept	T/C	Value	Debit	Credit	V	B
9	JD	01/07/2014	1200	O/Bal	Opening Balance	0	T9	4,840.20	4,840.20		-	-
52	SR	10/07/2014	MP01	BACS	Sales Receipt	0	T9	3,475.20	3,475.20		-	R
53	SR	13/07/2014	CC01	BACS	Sales Receipt	0	T9	1,772.35	1,772.35		-	R
54	SR	14/07/2014	AGC01	BACS	Sales Receipt	0	T9	4,210.32	4,210.32		-	R
55	SA	30/07/2014	AGC01	BACS	Payment on Account	0	T9	1,200.00	1,200.00		-	R
56	SR	24/07/2014	BGC01	Cheque	Sales Receipt	0	T9	1,269.60	1,269.60		-	R
57	PP	22/07/2014	SCS01	024229	Purchase Payment	0	T9	2,132.02		2,132.02	-	R
58	PP	23/07/2014	BW01	024230	Purchase Payment	0	T9	6,203.00		6,203.00	-	R
59	PP	23/07/2014	WW01	024231	Purchase Payment	0	T9	6,410.00		6,410.00	-	N
61	JD	29/07/2014	1200	TRANS	Bank Transfer	0	T9	3,000.00	3,000.00		-	R
62	BP	10/07/2014	1200	024226	Display table and shelving from	0	T1	1,340.00		1,340.00	N	R
63	BP	14/07/2014	1200	024227	Greetings cards for resale from	0	T1	299.00		299.00	N	R
64	BP	16/07/2014	1200	024228	Full page article in the Granby	0	T1	770.40		770.40	N	R
65	BP	15/07/2014	1200	DD	Granby Council business rates	0	T2	132.40		132.40	N	R
70	JC	11/07/2014	1200	024225	Restore the petty cash account	0	T9	48.24		48.24	-	R
74	SR	05/07/2014	AGC01	BACS	Sales Receipt	0	T9	856.80	856.80		-	R
75	BP	30/07/2014	1200	Charges	Bank charges	0	T2	22.00		22.00	N	R
							Totals:		20,624.47	17,357.06		
							History Balance:		3,267.41			

Purchase ledger (supplier) account for Burton Wholesale Only

Date: Time:				**Clifton Card Warehouse** **Supplier Activity (Detailed)**					Page:	1	
Date From: Date To:		01/01/1980 31/07/2014					Supplier From: Supplier To:		BW01 BW01		
Transaction From: Transaction To:		1 99,999,999					N/C From: N/C To:		 99999999		
Inc b/fwd transaction: Exc later payment:		No No					Dept From: Dept To:		0 999		

** NOTE: All report values are shown in Base Currency, unless otherwise indicated **

A/C:	BW01	Name:	Burton Wholesale		Contact:	Priya Malik		Tel:	0123 142124	

No	Type	Date	Ref	N/C	Details	Dept	T/C	Value	O/S	Debit	Credit	V	B
5	PI	01/07/2014	O/Bal	9998	Opening Balance	0	T9	6,203.00	0.00		6,203.00	-	-
51	PC	16/07/2014	36	5000	Purchase returns	0	T1	69.36 *	-69.36	69.36		N	-
58	PP	23/07/2014	024230	1200	Purchase Payment	0	T9	6,203.00	0.00	6,203.00		-	R
					Totals:			-69.36	-69.36	6,272.36	6,203.00		

Amount Outstanding	-69.36
Amount paid this period	6,203.00
Credit Limit £	12,300.00
Turnover YTD	6,145.20

Task 14 (continued)

Audit trail, showing full details of transactions

<table>
<tr><td colspan="2">Date:</td><td colspan="4" align="center">**Clifton Card Warehouse**</td><td colspan="2" align="right">Page: 1</td></tr>
<tr><td colspan="2">Time:</td><td colspan="4" align="center">**Audit Trail (Detailed)**</td><td colspan="2"></td></tr>
</table>

Date From:	01/01/1980	Customer From:
Date To:	31/12/2019	Customer To: ZZZZZZZZ
Transaction From:	1	Supplier From:
Transaction To:	99,999,999	Supplier To: ZZZZZZZZ
Exclude Deleted Tran:	No	

No	Type	A/C	N/C	Dp	Details	Date	Ref	Net	Tax	T/C	Pd	Paid	V	B	Bank Rec. Date
1	SI	AGC01				01/07/2014	O/Bal	4,210.32	0.00		Y	4,210.32	-		
		1	9998	0	Opening Balance			4,210.32	0.00	T9		4,210.32	-		
					4210.32 from SR 54	14/07/2014	BACS					4,210.32			
2	SI	BGC01				01/07/2014	O/Bal	262.50	0.00		N	0.00	-		
		2	9998	0	Opening Balance			262.50	0.00	T9		0.00	-		
3	SI	CC01				01/07/2014	O/Bal	1,798.75	0.00		Y	1,798.75	-		
		3	9998	0	Opening Balance			1,798.75	0.00	T9		1,798.75	-		
					26.40 from SC 45	08/07/2014	0074					26.40			
					1772.35 from SR 53	13/07/2014	BACS					1,772.35			
4	SI	MP01				01/07/2014	O/Bal	3,475.20	0.00		Y	3,475.20	-		
		4	9998	0	Opening Balance			3,475.20	0.00	T9		3,475.20	-		
					3475.20 from SR 52	10/07/2014	BACS					3,475.20			
5	PI	BW01				01/07/2014	O/Bal	6,203.00	0.00		Y	6,203.00	-		
		5	9998	0	Opening Balance			6,203.00	0.00	T9		6,203.00	-		
					6203.00 from PP 58	23/07/2014	024230					6,203.00			
6	PI	JFCS01				01/07/2014	O/Bal	2,004.24	0.00		N	0.00	-		
		6	9998	0	Opening Balance			2,004.24	0.00	T9		0.00	-		
7	PI	SCS01				01/07/2014	O/Bal	741.00	0.00		Y	741.00	-		
		7	9998	0	Opening Balance			741.00	0.00	T9		741.00	-		
					209.06 from PC 50	14/07/2014	CN41					209.06			
					531.94 from PP 57	22/07/2014	024229					531.94			
8	PI	WW01				01/07/2014	O/Bal	6,410.00	0.00		Y	6,410.00	-		
		8	9998	0	Opening Balance			6,410.00	0.00	T9		6,410.00	-		
					6410.00 from PP 59	23/07/2014	024231					6,410.00			
9	JD	1200				01/07/2014	O/Bal	4,840.20	0.00		Y	4,840.20	-	01/07/2014
		9	1200	0	Opening Balance			4,840.20	0.00	T9		4,840.20	-		
10	JC	9998				01/07/2014	O/Bal	4,840.20	0.00		Y	4,840.20	-		
		10	9998	0	Opening Balance			4,840.20	0.00	T9		4,840.20	-		
11	JD	1210				01/07/2014	O/Bal	6,000.00	0.00		Y	6,000.00	-	01/07/2014
		11	1210	0	Opening Balance			6,000.00	0.00	T9		6,000.00	-		
12	JC	9998				01/07/2014	O/Bal	6,000.00	0.00		Y	6,000.00	-		
		12	9998	0	Opening Balance			6,000.00	0.00	T9		6,000.00	-		
13	JD	1230				01/07/2014	O/Bal	50.00	0.00		Y	50.00	-	01/07/2014
		13	1230	0	Opening Balance			50.00	0.00	T9		50.00	-		
14	JC	9998				01/07/2014	O/Bal	50.00	0.00		Y	50.00	-		
		14	9998	0	Opening Balance			50.00	0.00	T9		50.00	-		
15	JC	2200				01/07/2014	O/Bal	8,780.00	0.00		Y	8,780.00	-		
		15	2200	0	Opening Balance			8,780.00	0.00	T9		8,780.00	-		
16	JD	9998				01/07/2014	O/Bal	8,780.00	0.00		Y	8,780.00	-		
		16	9998	0	Opening Balance			8,780.00	0.00	T9		8,780.00	-		
17	JD	2201				01/07/2014	O/Bal	1,640.00	0.00		Y	1,640.00	-		
		17	2201	0	Opening Balance			1,640.00	0.00	T9		1,640.00	-		
18	JC	9998				01/07/2014	O/Bal	1,640.00	0.00		Y	1,640.00	-		
		18	9998	0	Opening Balance			1,640.00	0.00	T9		1,640.00	-		
19	JD	0040				01/07/2014	O/Bal	34,650.00	0.00		Y	34,650.00	-		
		19	0040	0	Opening Balance			34,650.00	0.00	T9		34,650.00	-		
20	JC	9998				01/07/2014	O/Bal	34,650.00	0.00		Y	34,650.00	-		
		20	9998	0	Opening Balance			34,650.00	0.00	T9		34,650.00	-		
21	JC	3000				01/07/2014	O/Bal	10,000.00	0.00		Y	10,000.00	-		
		21	3000	0	Opening Balance			10,000.00	0.00	T9		10,000.00	-		
22	JD	9998				01/07/2014	O/Bal	10,000.00	0.00		Y	10,000.00	-		
		22	9998	0	Opening Balance			10,000.00	0.00	T9		10,000.00	-		
23	JC	4000				01/07/2014	O/Bal	8,741.25	0.00		Y	8,741.25	-		
		23	4000	0	Opening Balance			8,741.25	0.00	T9		8,741.25	-		

Date:							**Clifton Card Warehouse**							Page: 2	
Time:							**Audit Trail (Detailed)**								

No	Type	A/C	N/C	Dp	Details	Date	Ref	Net	Tax	T/C	Pd	Paid	V	B	Bank Rec. Date
24	JD	9998				01/07/2014	O/Bal	8,741.25	0.00		Y	8,741.25	-		
		24	9998	0	Opening Balance			8,741.25	0.00	T9		8,741.25	-		
25	JC	4001				01/07/2014	O/Bal	2,635.70	0.00		Y	2,635.70	-		
		25	4001	0	Opening Balance			2,635.70	0.00	T9		2,635.70	-		
26	JD	9998				01/07/2014	O/Bal	2,635.70	0.00		Y	2,635.70	-		
		26	9998	0	Opening Balance			2,635.70	0.00	T9		2,635.70	-		
27	JC	4002				01/07/2014	O/Bal	17,636.89	0.00		Y	17,636.89	-		
		27	4002	0	Opening Balance			17,636.89	0.00	T9		17,636.89	-		
28	JD	9998				01/07/2014	O/Bal	17,636.89	0.00		Y	17,636.89	-		
		28	9998	0	Opening Balance			17,636.89	0.00	T9		17,636.89	-		
29	JD	5000				01/07/2014	O/Bal	8,003.11	0.00		Y	8,003.11	-		
		29	5000	0	Opening Balance			8,003.11	0.00	T9		8,003.11	-		
30	JC	9998				01/07/2014	O/Bal	8,003.11	0.00		Y	8,003.11	-		
		30	9998	0	Opening Balance			8,003.11	0.00	T9		8,003.11	-		
31	JC	4906				01/07/2014	O/Bal	23.00	0.00		Y	23.00	-		
		31	4906	0	Opening Balance			23.00	0.00	T9		23.00	-		
32	JD	9998				01/07/2014	O/Bal	23.00	0.00		Y	23.00	-		
		32	9998	0	Opening Balance			23.00	0.00	T9		23.00	-		
33	JC	4904				01/07/2014	O/Bal	2,100.00	0.00		Y	2,100.00	-		
		33	4904	0	Opening Balance			2,100.00	0.00	T9		2,100.00	-		
34	JD	9998				01/07/2014	O/Bal	2,100.00	0.00		Y	2,100.00	-		
		34	9998	0	Opening Balance			2,100.00	0.00	T9		2,100.00	-		
35	JD	8200				01/07/2014	O/Bal	345.00	0.00		Y	345.00	-		
		35	8200	0	Opening Balance			345.00	0.00	T9		345.00	-		
36	JC	9998				01/07/2014	O/Bal	345.00	0.00		Y	345.00	-		
		36	9998	0	Opening Balance			345.00	0.00	T9		345.00	-		
37	SI	AGC01				02/07/2014	00895	714.00	142.80		Y	856.80	-		
		37	4001	0	x160 Rolls of wrapping paper			64.00	12.80	T1		76.80	N		
					76.80 from SR 74	05/07/2014	BACS					76.80			
		38	4002	0	x250 Packs of blue balloons			50.00	10.00	T1		60.00	N		
					60.00 from SR 74	05/07/2014	BACS					60.00			
		39	4002	0	x500 Packs of helium balloons			600.00	120.00	T1		720.00	N		
					720.00 from SR 74	05/07/2014	BACS					720.00			
40	SI	MP01				06/07/2014	00896	3,160.00	632.00		N	0.00	-		
		40	4000	0	x5000 Assorted greetings cards			3,100.00	620.00	T1		0.00	N		
		41	4002	0	x75 Banners			60.00	12.00	T1		0.00	N		
42	SI	BGC01				06/07/2014	00897	1,058.00	211.60		Y	1,269.60	-		
		42	4002	0	x205 Candles			123.00	24.60	T1		147.60	N		
					147.60 from SR 56	24/07/2014	Cheque					147.60			
		43	4002	0	x110 Table decorations			275.00	55.00	T1		330.00	N		
					330.00 from SR 56	24/07/2014	Cheque					330.00			
		44	4000	0	x300 Assorted greetings cards			660.00	132.00	T1		792.00	N		
					792.00 from SR 56	24/07/2014	Cheque					792.00			
45	SC	CC01				08/07/2014	0074	22.00	4.40		Y	26.40	-		
		45	4000	0	x10 Damaged greetings cards			22.00	4.40	T1		26.40	N		
					26.40 to SI 3	08/07/2014	O/Bal					26.40			
46	PI	JFCS01				03/07/2014	INV 3079	4,271.29	854.26		N	0.00	-		
		46	5000	0	Purchases			4,271.29	854.26	T1		0.00	N		
47	PI	WW01				10/07/2014	WW 417	2,970.05	594.01		N	0.00	-		
		47	5000	0	Purchases			2,970.05	594.01	T1		0.00	N		
48	PI	SCS01				12/07/2014	1784	1,333.40	266.68		Y	1,600.08	-		
		48	5000	0	Purchases			1,333.40	266.68	T1		1,600.08	N		
					1600.08 from PP 57	22/07/2014	024229					1,600.08			
49	PI	WW01				13/07/2014	32546	541.30	108.26		N	0.00	-		
		49	5000	0	Purchases			541.30	108.26	T1		0.00	N		
50	PC	SCS01				14/07/2014	CN41	174.22	34.84		Y	209.06	-		
		50	5000	0	Purchase returns			174.22	34.84	T1		209.06	N		
					209.06 to PI 7	14/07/2014	O/Bal					209.06			
51	PC	BW01				16/07/2014	36	57.80	11.56		N	0.00	-		
		51	5000	0	Purchase returns			57.80	11.56	T1		0.00	N		
52	SR	MP01				10/07/2014	BACS	3,475.20	0.00		Y	3,475.20	R		31/07/2014
		52	1200	0	Sales Receipt			3,475.20	0.00	T9		3,475.20	-		

Date:															

Clifton Card Warehouse
Audit Trail (Detailed)

Page: 3

No	Type	A/C	N/C	Dp	Details	Date	Ref	Net	Tax	T/C	Pd	Paid	V	B	Bank Rec. Date
					3475.20 to SI 4	10/07/2014	O/Bal					3,475.20			
53	SR	CC01				13/07/2014	BACS	1,772.35	0.00		Y	1,772.35	R		31/07/2014
		53	1200	0	Sales Receipt			1,772.35	0.00	T9		1,772.35	-		
					1772.35 to SI 3	13/07/2014	O/Bal					1,772.35			
54	SR	AGC01				14/07/2014	BACS	4,210.32	0.00		Y	4,210.32	R		31/07/2014
		54	1200	0	Sales Receipt			4,210.32	0.00	T9		4,210.32	-		
					4210.32 to SI 1	14/07/2014	O/Bal					4,210.32			
55	SA	AGC01				30/07/2014	BACS	1,200.00	0.00		N	0.00	R		31/07/2014
		55	1200	0	Payment on Account			1,200.00	0.00	T9		0.00	-		
56	SR	BGC01				24/07/2014	Cheque	1,269.60	0.00		Y	1,269.60	R		31/07/2014
		56	1200	0	Sales Receipt			1,269.60	0.00	T9		1,269.60	-		
					147.60 to SI 42	24/07/2014	00897					147.60			
					330.00 to SI 43	24/07/2014	00897					330.00			
					792.00 to SI 44	24/07/2014	00897					792.00			
57	PP	SCS01				22/07/2014	024229	2,132.02	0.00		Y	2,132.02	R		31/07/2014
		57	1200	0	Purchase Payment			2,132.02	0.00	T9		2,132.02	-		
					531.94 to PI 7	22/07/2014	O/Bal					531.94			
					1600.08 to PI 48	22/07/2014	1784					1,600.08			
58	PP	BW01				23/07/2014	024230	6,203.00	0.00		Y	6,203.00	R		31/07/2014
		58	1200	0	Purchase Payment			6,203.00	0.00	T9		6,203.00	-		
					6203.00 to PI 5	23/07/2014	O/Bal					6,203.00			
59	PP	WW01				23/07/2014	024231	6,410.00	0.00		Y	6,410.00	N		
		59	1200	0	Purchase Payment			6,410.00	0.00	T9		6,410.00	-		
					6410.00 to PI 8	23/07/2014	O/Bal					6,410.00			
60	JC	1210				29/07/2014	TRANS	3,000.00	0.00		Y	3,000.00	N		
		60	1210	0	Bank Transfer			3,000.00	0.00	T9		3,000.00	-		
61	JD	1200				29/07/2014	TRANS	3,000.00	0.00		Y	3,000.00	R		31/07/2014
		61	1200	0	Bank Transfer			3,000.00	0.00	T9		3,000.00	-		
62	BP	1200				10/07/2014	024226	1,116.67	223.33		Y	1,340.00	R		31/07/2014
		62	0040	0	Display table and shelving from			1,116.67	223.33	T1		1,340.00	-		
63	BP	1200				14/07/2014	024227	249.17	49.83		Y	299.00	R		31/07/2014
		63	5000	0	Greetings cards for resale from			249.17	49.83	T1		299.00	N		
64	BP	1200				16/07/2014	024228	642.00	128.40		Y	770.40	R		31/07/2014
		64	6201	0	Full page article in the Granby			642.00	128.40	T1		770.40	N		
65	BP	1200				15/07/2014	DD	132.40	0.00		Y	132.40	R		31/07/2014
		65	7103	0	Granby Council business rates			132.40	0.00	T2		132.40	N		
66	CP	1230				05/07/2014	054	10.17	2.03		Y	12.20	-		
		66	7801	0	Cleaning materials			10.17	2.03	T1		12.20	N		
67	CP	1230				06/07/2014	055	15.00	0.00		Y	15.00	-		
		67	8200	0	Donation to local charity			15.00	0.00	T9		15.00	-		
68	CP	1230				10/07/2014	056	14.80	0.00		Y	14.80	-		
		68	7400	0	Train ticket to promotional event			14.80	0.00	T2		14.80	N		
69	CP	1230				10/07/2014	057	5.20	1.04		Y	6.24	-		
		69	7502	0	Pack of printer paper			5.20	1.04	T1		6.24	N		
70	JC	1200				11/07/2014	024225	48.24	0.00		Y	48.24	R		31/07/2014
		70	1200	0	Restore the petty cash account			48.24	0.00	T9		48.24	-		
71	JD	1230				11/07/2014	024225	48.24	0.00		Y	48.24	-		
		71	1230	0	Restore the petty cash account			48.24	0.00	T9		48.24	-		
72	JD	0030				30/07/2014	012	3,748.00	0.00		Y	3,748.00	-		
		72	0030	0	Office equipment incorrectly			3,748.00	0.00	T9		3,748.00	-		
73	JC	0040				30/07/2014	012	3,748.00	0.00		Y	3,748.00	-		
		73	0040	0	Office equipment incorrectly			3,748.00	0.00	T9		3,748.00	-		
74	SR	AGC01				05/07/2014	BACS	856.80	0.00		Y	856.80	R		31/07/2014
		74	1200	0	Sales Receipt			856.80	0.00	T9		856.80	-		
					76.80 to SI 37	05/07/2014	00895					76.80			
					60.00 to SI 38	05/07/2014	00895					60.00			
					720.00 to SI 39	05/07/2014	00895					720.00			
75	BP	1200				30/07/2014	Charges	22.00	0.00		Y	22.00	R		31/07/2014
		75	7901	0	Bank charges			22.00	0.00	T2		22.00	N		

Practice assessment 4 answers

Task	Transaction Type	Account(s)		Date 20XX	Net Amount £	VAT £	Allocated against receipt/ Payment ✓	Reconciled with bank statement ✓
1	Customer O/bal	FC01		1 Aug	6,542.20		✓	
	Customer O/bal	FSS02		1 Aug	3,339.90		✓	
	Customer O/bal	NLC01		1 Aug	2,010.20		✓	
	Customer O/bal	NC02		1 Aug	7,542.00		✓	
2	Supplier O/bal	ROS01		1 Aug	4,350.00		✓	
	Supplier O/bal	SS01		1 Aug	2,230.00		✓	
	Supplier O/bal	TKAS01		1 Aug	3,740.60		✓	
	Supplier O/bal	WSL01		1 Aug	1,635.55			
3	Cr	Bank current account		1 Aug	2,403.00			✓
	Dr	Petty cash		1 Aug	100.00			
	Dr	Motor vehicles		1 Aug	8,730.50			
	Dr	Office equipment		1 Aug	12,707.70			
	Cr	Capital		1 Aug	10,000.00			
	Dr	Drawings		1 Aug	3,319.89			
	Cr	VAT on sales		1 Aug	6,502.40			
	Dr	VAT on purchases		1 Aug	1,870.46			
	Dr	Sales ledger control *		1 Aug	19,434.30			
	Cr	Purchase ledger control *		1 Aug	11,956.15			
	Cr	Sales – Ink		1 Aug	5,410.20			
	Cr	Sales – Paper		1 Aug	12,023.60			
	Cr	Sales – Filing and folders		1 Aug	3,704.65			
	Cr	Sales – General office supplies		1 Aug	8,945.04			
	Dr	Materials purchased		1 Aug	9,863.30			
	Dr	Telephone		1 Aug	208.00			
	Dr	Staff salaries		1 Aug	3,641.00			
	Dr	Vehicle insurance		1 Aug	652.89			
	Dr	Electricity		1 Aug	230.00			
	Dr	Vehicle		1 Aug	187.00			
		*If appropriate						
4	Sales inv	NC02	Sales:	2 Aug				
			General office supplies		375.00	75.00	✓	
			Paper		1,274.00	254.80	✓	
			Filing and folders		2,100.00	420.00	✓	
	Sales CN	FC01	Sales:	6 Aug				
			Ink		174.00	34.80	✓	
			Filing and folders		21.00	4.20	✓	
	Sales inv	FSS02	Sales:	14 Aug				
			Paper		59.80	11.96		
			Paper		59.80	11.96		
			General office supplies		210.00	42.00		
			Ink		2,230.00	446.00		
	Sales CN	NC02	Sales:	16 Aug				
			General office supplies		17.50	3.50	✓	
			Paper		45.50	9.10	✓	
5	Purchase inv	TKAS01	Office equipment	8 Aug	1,161.20	232.24	✓	
	Purchase inv	WSL01	Repairs and renewals	9 Aug	6.90	1.38		
			Advertising		351.96	70.39		
	Purchase inv	SS01	Purchases	11 Aug	15,740.30	3,148.06	✓	
	Purchase CN	SS01	Purchases	15 Aug	3,541.20	708.24	✓	

No.	Type	Account	Details	Date	Amount	VAT		
6	Customer receipt	NC02	Bank	20 Aug	11,965.20		✓	✓
	Customer receipt	NLC01	Bank	21 Aug	2,010.20		✓	✓
	Customer receipt	FC01	Bank	12 Aug	6,308.20		✓	✓
	Customer receipt	FSS02	Bank	12 Aug	3,339.90		✓	✓
	Customer receipt	FSS02	Bank	18 Aug	2,400.00			✓
7	Supplier payment	ROS01	Bank	22 Aug	4,350.00		✓	✓
	Supplier payment	SS01	Bank	22 Aug	16,868.92		✓	✓
	Supplier payment	WSL01	Bank	22 Aug	5,000.00			✓
	Supplier payment	TKAS01	Bank	14 Aug	5,134.04		✓	✓
8	Bank payment	Bank	Recruitment	14 Aug	575.00	115.00		✓
	Bank payment	Bank	Telephone	30 Aug	65.00	13.00		
	Bank receipt	Bank	Sales – General Office Supplies	18 Aug	331.67	66.33		✓
	Bank receipt	Bank	Loan	13 Aug	20,000.00			
	Dr	Bank Deposit		27 Aug	15,000.00			✓
	Cr	Bank Current		27 Aug	15,000.00			✓
9	Bank payment	Bank	Office equipment maintenance – DD	24 Aug	72.60	14.52		✓
	Bank receipt	Bank	Rental Income	25 Aug	320.00	64.00		✓
10	Dr	Petty cash		2 Aug	50.00			
	Cr	Bank		2 Aug	50.00			✓
	Cash payment	Petty cash	Postage	2 Aug	6.36			
	Cash payment	Petty cash	Miscellaneous expenses	5 Aug	22.10	4.42		
	Cash payment	Petty cash	Miscellaneous expenses	8 Aug	6.92	1.38		
11	Journal debit	Sales - Ink		12 Aug	64.80			
	Journal credit	Sales – General office supplies		12 Aug	64.80			
11	Journal debit	Drawings		20 Aug	350.00			
	Journal credit	Materials purchased		20 Aug	350.00			
12	Bank payment	Bank	Bank charges	30 Aug	40.00			✓

Task 6

Fusion Stationery Supplies Statement of account

Southglade Stationery Warehouse
Unit 3
810 Southglade Road
Newbridge
NE6 6RB

FSS02

Fusion Stationery Supplies   30/08/2014
94 Bracebridge Road

Filey

FL6 1BD

All values are shown in Pound Sterling

01/08/2014	O/Bal	Goods/Services	£	3,339.90			£	3,339.90
14/08/2014	007141	Goods/Services	£	3,071.52			£	6,411.42
12/08/2014	BACS	Payment			£	3,339.90	£	3,071.52
18/08/2014	BACS	Payment			£	2,400.00	£	671.52

| £ | 671.52 | £ | 0.00 | £ | 0.00 | £ | 0.00 | £ | 0.00 | £ | 671.52 |

Task 7

Riverside Office Supplies Ltd Remittance Advice

Southglade Stationery Warehouse
Unit 3
810 Southglade Road
Newbridge
NE6 6RB

To	ROS01

Riverside Office Supplies Ltd
52 Riverside Way

Filey

FG1 2NP

Date 22/08/2014

Cheque No BACS

REMITTANCE ADVICE

NOTE: All values are shown in Pound Sterling

Date	Ref. #	Details	Debit	Credit
01/08/2014	O/Bal	Opening Balance		£ 4,350.00

Amount Paid

£ 4,350.00

Task 9

First recurring entry

Add / Edit Recurring Entry ✕

Recurring Entry From / To

Bank A/C	1200	Bank Current Account
Nominal Code	7701	Office Machine Maintenance

Recurring Entry Details

Transaction Type	Bank/Cash/Credit Card Payment
Transaction Ref	DD
Transaction Details	PH Photocopiers maintenance
Department	0

Posting Frequency

Every	1 Month(s)	Total Required Postings	10
Start Date	24/08/2014	Finish Date	24/05/2015
Next Posting Date	24/08/2014	Suspend Posting ?	☐
Last Posted			

Posting Amounts

Net Amount 72.60   Tax Code T1 20.00   VAT 14.52

OK   Cancel

Second recurring entry

Add / Edit Recurring Entry ✕

Recurring Entry From / To

Bank A/C To	1200	Bank Current Account
Nominal Code	4904	Rent Income

Recurring Entry Details

Transaction Type	Bank/Cash/Credit Card Receipt
Transaction Ref	STO
Transaction Details	Rental income from Harris Removals
Department	0

Posting Frequency

Every	1 Month(s)	Total Required Postings	6
Start Date	25/08/2014	Finish Date	25/01/2015
Next Posting Date	25/08/2014	Suspend Posting ?	☐
Last Posted			

Posting Amounts

Net Amount 320.00   Tax Code T1 20.00   VAT 64.00

OK   Cancel

Task 13

(a)

Backup

Backup dialog box

Tabs: Backup Company | Advanced Options | Previous Backups

Company Details

You are about to create a backup of:

Company Name: Southglade Stationery Warehouse

Found In: C:\PROGRAMDATA\SAGE\ACCOUNTS\2012\COMPANY.000\

Where do you want the company backed up to?

Please click Browse to select a location to save this backup to. We have suggested a filename for this backup. If you are happy with this suggestion, click OK to save the backup.

Backing Up to removable media? Insert the device before clicking OK.

Backing Up to CD? Refer to the Help now.

Filename : SSWbackup

Location : F:\

Browse...

OK   Cancel   Help

(b)

Change password

Change Password dialog box

Logon Name   MANAGER

New Password   xxxxxxx

Confirm New Password   xxxxxxx

Discard   OK   Cancel

Task 14

Purchase returns day book (Supplier credit notes)

| Date:
Time: | | | | Southglade Stationery Warehouse
Day Books: Supplier Credits (Summary) | | | | | Page: | 1 |

Date From: Date To:	01/01/1980 31/12/2019						Supplier From: Supplier To:			ZZZZZZZZ

Transaction From: 1
Transaction To: 99,999,999

Tran No.	Item	Type	Date	A/C Ref	Inv Ref	Details	Net Amount	Tax Amount	Gross Amount
60	1	PC	15/08/2014	SS01	124	Damaged goods returned	3,541.20	708.24	4,249.44
						Totals	3,541.20	708.24	4,249.44

Aged trade payables analysis

| Date:
Time: | | Southglade Stationery Warehouse
Aged Creditors Analysis (Summary) | | | | Page: | 1 |

Report Date: 31/08/2014
Include future transactions: No
Exclude Later Payments: No

Supplier From:
Supplier To: ZZZZZZZZ

** NOTE: All report values are shown in Base Currency, unless otherwise indicated **

A/C	Name		Credit Limit	Turnover	Balance	Future	Current	Period 1	Period 2	Period 3	Older
WSL01	Wilford & Son Ltd	£	4,200.00	1,994.41	-2,933.82	0.00	-4,569.37	1,635.55	0.00	0.00	0.00
		Totals:		1,994.41	-2,933.82	0.00	-4,569.37	1,635.55	0.00	0.00	0.00

Sales day book (Customer Invoices)

| Date:
Time: | | | | Southglade Stationery Warehouse
Day Books: Customer Invoices (Summary) | | | | Page: | 1 |

Date From: Date To:	01/01/1980 31/12/2019						Customer From: Customer To:		ZZZZZZZZ

Transaction From: 1
Transaction To: 99,999,999

Tran No.	Items	Tp	Date	A/C Ref	Inv Ref	Details	Net Amount	Tax Amount	Gross Amount
1	1	SI	01/08/2014	FC01	O/Bal	Opening Balance	6,542.20	0.00	6,542.20
2	1	SI	01/08/2014	FSS02	O/Bal	Opening Balance	3,339.90	0.00	3,339.90
3	1	SI	01/08/2014	NLC01	O/Bal	Opening Balance	2,010.20	0.00	2,010.20
4	1	SI	01/08/2014	NC02	O/Bal	Opening Balance	7,542.00	0.00	7,542.00
45	3	SI	02/08/2014	NC02	007140	Black pens	3,749.00	749.80	4,498.80
50	4	SI	14/08/2014	FSS02	007141	Blue paper	2,559.60	511.92	3,071.52
						Totals:	25,742.90	1,261.72	27,004.62

Trial balance as at 31 August 20XX

Date:	Southglade Stationery Warehouse		Page:	1
Time:	Period Trial Balance			

To Period: Month 1, August 2014

N/C	Name	Debit	Credit
0030	Office Equipment	13,868.90	
0050	Motor Vehicles	8,730.50	
1100	Debtors Control Account	671.52	
1200	Bank Current Account		2,895.58
1210	Bank Deposit Account	15,000.00	
1230	Petty Cash	108.82	
2100	Creditors Control Account	2,933.82	
2200	Sales Tax Control Account		7,842.85
2201	Purchase Tax Control Account	4,762.61	
2300	Loans		20,000.00
3000	Capital		10,000.00
3050	Drawings	3,669.89	
4000	Sales - Ink		7,401.40
4001	Sales - Paper		13,371.70
4002	Sales - Filing and folders		5,783.65
4003	Sales - General office supplies		9,909.01
4904	Rent Income		320.00
5000	Materials Purchased	21,712.40	
6201	Advertising	351.96	
6900	Miscellaneous Expenses	29.02	
7003	Staff Salaries	3,641.00	
7008	Recruitment Expenses	575.00	
7200	Electricity	230.00	
7300	Vehicle Fuel	187.00	
7303	Vehicle Insurance	652.89	
7501	Postage and Carriage	6.36	
7550	Telephone and Fax	273.00	
7701	Office Machine Maintenance	72.60	
7800	Repairs and Renewals	6.90	
7901	Bank Charges	40.00	
	Totals:	77,524.19	77,524.19

Task 14 (continued)

All sales ledger (customer) accounts

Date:				Southglade Stationery Warehouse				Page:	1
Time:				**Customer Activity (Detailed)**					

Date From:	01/01/1980			Customer From:		
Date To:	31/08/2014			Customer To:	ZZZZZZZZ	
Transaction From:	1			N/C From:		
Transaction To:	99,999,999			N/C To:	99999999	
Inc b/fwd transaction:	No			Dept From:	0	
Exc later payment:	No			Dept To:	999	

** NOTE: All report values are shown in Base Currency, unless otherwise indicated **

A/C:	FC01	Name:	Farnsworth College		Contact:	David Roberts		Tel:	0198 332113

No	Type	Date	Ref	N/C	Details	Dept	T/C	Value	O/S	Debit	Credit	V	B
1	SI	01/08/2014	O/Bal	9998	Opening Balance	0	T9	6,542.20		6,542.20		-	-
48	SC	06/08/2014	047	4000	Ink cartridges returned	0	T1	208.80			208.80	N	-
49	SC	06/08/2014	047	4002	Folders returned	0	T1	25.20			25.20	N	-
63	SR	12/08/2014	BACS	1200	Sales Receipt	0	T9	6,308.20			6,308.20	-	R
					Totals:			0.00	0.00	6,542.20	6,542.20		

Amount Outstanding	0.00
Amount Paid this period	6,308.20
Credit Limit £	9,000.00
Turnover YTD	6,347.20

A/C:	FSS02	Name:	Fusion Stationery Supplies		Contact:	Janet Spencer		Tel:	0150 963424

No	Type	Date	Ref	N/C	Details	Dept	T/C	Value	O/S	Debit	Credit	V	B
2	SI	01/08/2014	O/Bal	9998	Opening Balance	0	T9	3,339.90		3,339.90		-	-
50	SI	14/08/2014	007141	4001	Blue paper	0	T1	71.76 *	71.76	71.76		N	-
51	SI	14/08/2014	007141	4001	Green paper	0	T1	71.76 *	71.76	71.76		N	-
52	SI	14/08/2014	007141	4003	Highlighter pens	0	T1	252.00 *	252.00	252.00		N	-
53	SI	14/08/2014	007141	4000	Ink cartridges	0	T1	2,676.00 *	2,676.00	2,676.00		N	-
64	SR	12/08/2014	BACS	1200	Sales Receipt	0	T9	3,339.90			3,339.90	-	R
65	SA	18/08/2014	BACS	1200	Payment on Account	0	T9	2,400.00 *	-2,400.00		2,400.00	-	R
					Totals:			671.52	671.52	6,411.42	5,739.90		

Amount Outstanding	671.52
Amount Paid this period	5,739.90
Credit Limit £	22,000.00
Turnover YTD	5,899.50

A/C:	NC02	Name:	Northgate College		Contact:	Lukasz Cservenyak		Tel:	0150 077360

No	Type	Date	Ref	N/C	Details	Dept	T/C	Value	O/S	Debit	Credit	V	B
4	SI	01/08/2014	O/Bal	9998	Opening Balance	0	T9	7,542.00		7,542.00		-	-
45	SI	02/08/2014	007140	4003	Black pens	0	T1	450.00		450.00		N	-
46	SI	02/08/2014	007140	4001	A4 paper	0	T1	1,528.80		1,528.80		N	-
47	SI	02/08/2014	007140	4002	Lever arch folders	0	T1	2,520.00		2,520.00		N	-
54	SC	16/08/2014	048	4003	Black pens returned	0	T1	21.00			21.00	N	-
55	SC	16/08/2014	048	4001	Paper returned	0	T1	54.60			54.60	N	-
61	SR	20/08/2014	Cheque	1200	Sales Receipt	0	T9	11,965.20			11,965.20	-	R
					Totals:			0.00	0.00	12,040.80	12,040.80		

Amount Outstanding	0.00
Amount Paid this period	11,965.20
Credit Limit £	12,100.00
Turnover YTD	11,228.00

A/C:	NLC01	Name:	Newbridge Learning Centre		Contact:	Samuel Impellizzeri		Tel:	0198 213452

No	Type	Date	Ref	N/C	Details	Dept	T/C	Value	O/S	Debit	Credit	V	B
3	SI	01/08/2014	O/Bal	9998	Opening Balance	0	T9	2,010.20		2,010.20		-	-
62	SR	21/08/2014	Cheque	1200	Sales Receipt	0	T9	2,010.20			2,010.20	-	R
					Totals:			0.00	0.00	2,010.20	2,010.20		

Amount Outstanding	0.00
Amount Paid this period	2,010.20
Credit Limit £	8,250.00
Turnover YTD	2,010.20

All purchase ledger (supplier) accounts

Date:					**Southglade Stationery Warehouse**				Page:	1
Time:					**Supplier Activity (Detailed)**					

Date From:	01/01/1980					Supplier From:	
Date To:	31/08/2014					Supplier To:	ZZZZZZZZ
Transaction From:	1					N/C From:	
Transaction To:	99,999,999					N/C To:	99999999
Inc b/fwd transaction:	No					Dept From:	0
Exc later payment:	No					Dept To:	999

** NOTE: All report values are shown in Base Currency, unless otherwise indicated **

A/C: ROS01 **Name:** Riverside Office Supplies Ltd   **Contact:** Catherine Hemmingway   **Tel:** 0150 210210

No	Type	Date	Ref	N/C	Details	Dept	T/C	Value	O/S	Debit	Credit	V	B
5	PI	01/08/2014	O/Bal	9998	Opening Balance	0	T9	4,350.00	0.00		4,350.00	-	-
66	PP	22/08/2014	BACS	1200	Purchase Payment	0	T9	4,350.00	0.00	4,350.00		-	R
					Totals:			0.00	0.00	4,350.00	4,350.00		

Amount Outstanding	0.00
Amount paid this period	4,350.00
Credit Limit £	6,400.00
Turnover YTD	4,350.00

A/C: SS01 **Name:** Shelford Stationery   **Contact:** Louise Richards   **Tel:** 0197 113679

No	Type	Date	Ref	N/C	Details	Dept	T/C	Value	O/S	Debit	Credit	V	B
6	PI	01/08/2014	O/Bal	9998	Opening Balance	0	T9	2,230.00	0.00		2,230.00	-	-
59	PI	11/08/2014	012012	5000	Goods for resale	0	T1	18,888.36	0.00		18,888.36	N	-
60	PC	15/08/2014	124	5000	Damaged goods returned	0	T1	4,249.44	0.00	4,249.44		N	-
67	PP	22/08/2014	BACS	1200	Purchase Payment	0	T9	16,868.92	0.00	16,868.92		-	R
					Totals:			0.00	0.00	21,118.36	21,118.36		

Amount Outstanding	0.00
Amount paid this period	16,868.92
Credit Limit £	22,000.00
Turnover YTD	14,429.10

A/C: TKAS01 **Name:** TKA Supplies   **Contact:** Tamara Tomlinson   **Tel:** 0121 669774

No	Type	Date	Ref	N/C	Details	Dept	T/C	Value	O/S	Debit	Credit	V	B
7	PI	01/08/2014	O/Bal	9998	Opening Balance	0	T9	3,740.60	0.00		3,740.60	-	-
56	PI	08/08/2014	INV635	0030	Computers	0	T1	1,393.44	0.00		1,393.44	N	-
69	PP	14/08/2014	201635	1200	Purchase Payment	0	T9	5,134.04	0.00	5,134.04		-	R
					Totals:			0.00	0.00	5,134.04	5,134.04		

Amount Outstanding	0.00
Amount paid this period	5,134.04
Credit Limit £	5,500.00
Turnover YTD	4,901.80

A/C: WSL01 **Name:** Wilford & Son Ltd   **Contact:** Ron Wilford   **Tel:** 0150 200300

No	Type	Date	Ref	N/C	Details	Dept	T/C	Value	O/S	Debit	Credit	V	B
8	PI	01/08/2014	O/Bal	9998	Opening Balance	0	T9	1,635.55 *	1,635.55		1,635.55	-	-
57	PI	09/08/2014	6310	7800	Filing cabinet locks	0	T1	8.28 *	8.28		8.28	N	-
58	PI	09/08/2014	6310	6201	Promotional stands	0	T1	422.35 *	422.35		422.35	N	-
68	PA	22/08/2014	BACS	1200	Payment on Account	0	T9	5,000.00 *	-5,000.00	5,000.00		-	R
					Totals:			-2,933.82	-2,933.82	5,000.00	2,066.18		

Amount Outstanding	-2,933.82
Amount paid this period	5,000.00
Credit Limit £	4,200.00
Turnover YTD	1,994.41

Task 14 (continued)

The Sales – General office supplies account in the nominal ledger

Date:										Page:	1	

Southglade Stationery Warehouse
Nominal Activity

Date From:	01/01/1980							N/C From:	4003
Date To:	31/08/2014							N/C To:	4003

Transaction From: 1
Transaction To: 99,999,999

N/C:	4003		Name:	Sales - General office supplies			Account Balance:		9,909.01 CR

No	Type	Date	Account	Ref	Details	Dept	T/C	Value	Debit	Credit	V	B
31	JC	01/08/2014	4003	O/Bal	Opening Balance	0	T9	8,945.04		8,945.04	-	-
45	SI	02/08/2014	NC02	007140	Black pens	0	T1	375.00		375.00	N	-
52	SI	14/08/2014	FSS02	007141	Highlighter pens	0	T1	210.00		210.00	N	-
54	SC	16/08/2014	NC02	048	Black pens returned	0	T1	17.50	17.50		N	-
72	BR	18/08/2014	1200	94	Calculators	0	T1	331.67		331.67	N	R
84	JC	12/08/2014	4003	017	Correction of error	0	T9	64.80		64.80	-	-
							Totals:		17.50	9,926.51		
							History Balance:			9,909.01		

Audit trail, showing full details of transactions

Date:							Southglade Stationery Warehouse					Page:	1
Time:							**Audit Trail (Detailed)**						

Date From:	01/01/1980		Customer From:	
Date To:	31/12/2019		Customer To:	ZZZZZZZZ
Transaction From:	1		Supplier From:	
Transaction To:	99,999,999		Supplier To:	ZZZZZZZZ

Exclude Deleted Tran: No

No	Type	A/C	N/C	Dp	Details	Date	Ref	Net	Tax	T/C	Pd	Paid	V	B	Bank Rec. Date
1	SI	FC01				01/08/2014	O/Bal	6,542.20	0.00		Y	6,542.20	-		
		1	9998	0	Opening Balance			6,542.20	0.00	T9		6,542.20	-		
					208.80 from SC 48	06/08/2014	047					208.80			
					25.20 from SC 49	06/08/2014	047					25.20			
					6308.20 from SR 63	12/08/2014	BACS					6,308.20			
2	SI	FSS02				01/08/2014	O/Bal	3,339.90	0.00		Y	3,339.90	-		
		2	9998	0	Opening Balance			3,339.90	0.00	T9		3,339.90	-		
					3339.90 from SR 64	12/08/2014	BACS					3,339.90			
3	SI	NLC01				01/08/2014	O/Bal	2,010.20	0.00		Y	2,010.20	-		
		3	9998	0	Opening Balance			2,010.20	0.00	T9		2,010.20	-		
					2010.20 from SR 62	21/08/2014	Cheque					2,010.20			
4	SI	NC02				01/08/2014	O/Bal	7,542.00	0.00		Y	7,542.00	-		
		4	9998	0	Opening Balance			7,542.00	0.00	T9		7,542.00	-		
					21.00 from SC 54	16/08/2014	048					21.00			
					54.60 from SC 55	16/08/2014	048					54.60			
					7466.40 from SR 61	20/08/2014	Cheque					7,466.40			
5	PI	ROS01				01/08/2014	O/Bal	4,350.00	0.00		Y	4,350.00	-		
		5	9998	0	Opening Balance			4,350.00	0.00	T9		4,350.00	-		
					4350.00 from PP 66	22/08/2014	BACS					4,350.00			
6	PI	SS01				01/08/2014	O/Bal	2,230.00	0.00		Y	2,230.00	-		
		6	9998	0	Opening Balance			2,230.00	0.00	T9		2,230.00	-		
					2230.00 from PC 60	15/08/2014	124					2,230.00			
7	PI	TKAS01				01/08/2014	O/Bal	3,740.60	0.00		Y	3,740.60	-		
		7	9998	0	Opening Balance			3,740.60	0.00	T9		3,740.60	-		
					3740.60 from PP 69	14/08/2014	201635					3,740.60			
8	PI	WSL01				01/08/2014	O/Bal	1,635.55	0.00		N	0.00	-		
		8	9998	0	Opening Balance			1,635.55	0.00	T9		0.00	-		
9	JC	1200				01/08/2014	O/Bal	2,403.00	0.00		Y	2,403.00	-		01/08/2014
		9	1200	0	Opening Balance			2,403.00	0.00	T9		2,403.00	-		
10	JD	9998				01/08/2014	O/Bal	2,403.00	0.00		Y	2,403.00	-		
		10	9998	0	Opening Balance			2,403.00	0.00	T9		2,403.00	-		
11	JD	1230				01/08/2014	O/Bal	100.00	0.00		Y	100.00	-		01/08/2014
		11	1230	0	Opening Balance			100.00	0.00	T9		100.00	-		
12	JC	9998				01/08/2014	O/Bal	100.00	0.00		Y	100.00	-		
		12	9998	0	Opening Balance			100.00	0.00	T9		100.00	-		
13	JD	0050				01/08/2014	O/Bal	8,730.50	0.00		Y	8,730.50	-		
		13	0050	0	Opening Balance			8,730.50	0.00	T9		8,730.50	-		
14	JC	9998				01/08/2014	O/Bal	8,730.50	0.00		Y	8,730.50	-		
		14	9998	0	Opening Balance			8,730.50	0.00	T9		8,730.50	-		
15	JD	0030				01/08/2014	O/Bal	12,707.70	0.00		Y	12,707.70	-		
		15	0030	0	Opening Balance			12,707.70	0.00	T9		12,707.70	-		
16	JC	9998				01/08/2014	O/Bal	12,707.70	0.00		Y	12,707.70	-		
		16	9998	0	Opening Balance			12,707.70	0.00	T9		12,707.70	-		
17	JC	3000				01/08/2014	O/Bal	10,000.00	0.00		Y	10,000.00	-		
		17	3000	0	Opening Balance			10,000.00	0.00	T9		10,000.00	-		
18	JD	9998				01/08/2014	O/Bal	10,000.00	0.00		Y	10,000.00	-		
		18	9998	0	Opening Balance			10,000.00	0.00	T9		10,000.00	-		
19	JD	3050				01/08/2014	O/Bal	3,319.89	0.00		Y	3,319.89	-		
		19	3050	0	Opening Balance			3,319.89	0.00	T9		3,319.89	-		
20	JC	9998				01/08/2014	O/Bal	3,319.89	0.00		Y	3,319.89	-		
		20	9998	0	Opening Balance			3,319.89	0.00	T9		3,319.89	-		
21	JC	2200				01/08/2014	O/Bal	6,502.40	0.00		Y	6,502.40	-		
		21	2200	0	Opening Balance			6,502.40	0.00	T9		6,502.40	-		

No	Tp	A/C	N/C	Dept	Details	Date	Ref	Net	Tax	T/C	Pd	Amount
22	JD	9998				01/08/2014	O/Bal	6,502.40	0.00		Y	6,502.40 -
		22	9998	0	Opening Balance			6,502.40	0.00	T9		6,502.40 -
23	JD	2201				01/08/2014	O/Bal	1,870.46	0.00		Y	1,870.46 -
		23	2201	0	Opening Balance			1,870.46	0.00	T9		1,870.46 -
24	JC	9998				01/08/2014	O/Bal	1,870.46	0.00		Y	1,870.46 -
		24	9998	0	Opening Balance			1,870.46	0.00	T9		1,870.46 -
25	JC	4000				01/08/2014	O/Bal	5,410.20	0.00		Y	5,410.20 -
		25	4000	0	Opening Balance			5,410.20	0.00	T9		5,410.20 -
26	JD	9998				01/08/2014	O/Bal	5,410.20	0.00		Y	5,410.20 -
		26	9998	0	Opening Balance			5,410.20	0.00	T9		5,410.20 -
27	JC	4001				01/08/2014	O/Bal	12,023.60	0.00		Y	12,023.60 -
		27	4001	0	Opening Balance			12,023.60	0.00	T9		12,023.60 -
28	JD	9998				01/08/2014	O/Bal	12,023.60	0.00		Y	12,023.60 -
		28	9998	0	Opening Balance			12,023.60	0.00	T9		12,023.60 -
29	JC	4002				01/08/2014	O/Bal	3,704.65	0.00		Y	3,704.65 -
		29	4002	0	Opening Balance			3,704.65	0.00	T9		3,704.65 -
30	JD	9998				01/08/2014	O/Bal	3,704.65	0.00		Y	3,704.65 -
		30	9998	0	Opening Balance			3,704.65	0.00	T9		3,704.65 -
31	JC	4003				01/08/2014	O/Bal	8,945.04	0.00		Y	8,945.04 -
		31	4003	0	Opening Balance			8,945.04	0.00	T9		8,945.04 -
32	JD	9998				01/08/2014	O/Bal	8,945.04	0.00		Y	8,945.04 -
		32	9998	0	Opening Balance			8,945.04	0.00	T9		8,945.04 -
33	JD	5000				01/08/2014	O/Bal	9,863.30	0.00		Y	9,863.30 -
		33	5000	0	Opening Balance			9,863.30	0.00	T9		9,863.30 -
34	JC	9998				01/08/2014	O/Bal	9,863.30	0.00		Y	9,863.30 -
		34	9998	0	Opening Balance			9,863.30	0.00	T9		9,863.30 -
35	JD	7550				01/08/2014	O/Bal	208.00	0.00		Y	208.00 -
		35	7550	0	Opening Balance			208.00	0.00	T9		208.00 -
36	JC	9998				01/08/2014	O/Bal	208.00	0.00		Y	208.00 -
		36	9998	0	Opening Balance			208.00	0.00	T9		208.00 -
37	JD	7003				01/08/2014	O/Bal	3,641.00	0.00		Y	3,641.00 -
		37	7003	0	Opening Balance			3,641.00	0.00	T9		3,641.00 -
38	JC	9998				01/08/2014	O/Bal	3,641.00	0.00		Y	3,641.00 -
		38	9998	0	Opening Balance			3,641.00	0.00	T9		3,641.00 -
39	JD	7303				01/08/2014	O/Bal	652.89	0.00		Y	652.89 -
		39	7303	0	Opening Balance			652.89	0.00	T9		652.89 -
40	JC	9998				01/08/2014	O/Bal	652.89	0.00		Y	652.89 -
		40	9998	0	Opening Balance			652.89	0.00	T9		652.89 -
41	JD	7200				01/08/2014	O/Bal	230.00	0.00		Y	230.00 -
		41	7200	0	Opening Balance			230.00	0.00	T9		230.00 -
42	JC	9998				01/08/2014	O/Bal	230.00	0.00		Y	230.00 -
		42	9998	0	Opening Balance			230.00	0.00	T9		230.00 -
43	JD	7300				01/08/2014	O/Bal	187.00	0.00		Y	187.00 -
		43	7300	0	Opening Balance			187.00	0.00	T9		187.00 -
44	JC	9998				01/08/2014	O/Bal	187.00	0.00		Y	187.00 -
		44	9998	0	Opening Balance			187.00	0.00	T9		187.00 -
45	SI	NC02				02/08/2014	007140	3,749.00	749.80		Y	4,498.80 -
		45	4003	0	Black pens			375.00	75.00	T1		450.00
					450.00 from SR 61	20/08/2014	Cheque					450.00
		46	4001	0	A4 paper			1,274.00	254.80	T1		1,528.80
					1528.80 from SR 61	20/08/2014	Cheque					1,528.80
		47	4002	0	Lever arch folders			2,100.00	420.00	T1		2,520.00 N
					2520.00 from SR 61	20/08/2014	Cheque					2,520.00
48	SC	FC01				06/08/2014	047	195.00	39.00		Y	234.00 -
		48	4000	0	Ink cartridges returned			174.00	34.80	T1		208.80 N
					208.80 to SI 1	06/08/2014	O/Bal					208.80
		49	4002	0	Folders returned			21.00	4.20	T1		25.20 N
					25.20 to SI 1	06/08/2014	O/Bal					25.20
50	SI	FSS02				14/08/2014	007141	2,559.60	511.92		N	0.00 -
		50	4001	0	Blue paper			59.80	11.96	T1		0.00 N
		51	4001	0	Green paper			59.80	11.96	T1		0.00 N
		52	4003	0	Highlighter pens			210.00	42.00	T1		0.00 N
		53	4000	0	Ink cartidges			2,230.00	446.00	T1		0.00 N
54	SC	NC02				16/08/2014	048	63.00	12.60		Y	75.60 -
		54	4003	0	Black pens returned			17.50	3.50	T1		21.00 N
					21.00 to SI 4	16/08/2014	O/Bal					21.00
		55	4001	0	Paper returned			45.50	9.10	T1		54.60 N
					54.60 to SI 4	16/08/2014	O/Bal					54.60
56	PI	TKAS01				08/08/2014	INV635	1,161.20	232.24		Y	1,393.44 -
		56	0030	0	Computers			1,161.20	232.24	T1		1,393.44 N
					1393.44 from PP 69	14/08/2014	201635					1,393.44

57	PI	WSL01					09/08/2014 6310		358.86	71.77	N		0.00	-	
		57	7800	0	Filing cabinet locks				6.90	1.38 T1			0.00	N	
		58	6201	0	Promotional stands				351.96	70.39 T1			0.00	N	
59	PI	SS01					11/08/2014 012012		15,740.30	3,148.06	Y		18,888.36	-	
		59	5000	0	Goods for resale				15,740.30	3,148.06 T1			18,888.36	N	
					2019.44 from PC 60	15/08/2014 124							2,019.44		
					16868.92 from PP 67	22/08/2014 BACS							16,868.92		
60	PC	SS01					15/08/2014 124		3,541.20	708.24	Y		4,249.44	-	
		60	5000	0	Damaged goods returned				3,541.20	708.24 T1			4,249.44	N	
					2230.00 to PI 6	15/08/2014 O/Bal							2,230.00		
					2019.44 to PI 59	15/08/2014 012012							2,019.44		
61	SR	NC02					20/08/2014 Cheque		11,965.20	0.00	Y		11,965.20	R	31/08/2014
		61	1200	0	Sales Receipt				11,965.20	0.00 T9			11,965.20	-	
					7466.40 to SI 4	20/08/2014 O/Bal							7,466.40		
					450.00 to SI 45	20/08/2014 007140							450.00		
					1528.80 to SI 46	20/08/2014 007140							1,528.80		
					2520.00 to SI 47	20/08/2014 007140							2,520.00		
62	SR	NLC01					21/08/2014 Cheque		2,010.20	0.00	Y		2,010.20	R	31/08/2014
		62	1200	0	Sales Receipt				2,010.20	0.00 T9			2,010.20	-	
					2010.20 to SI 3	21/08/2014 O/Bal							2,010.20		
63	SR	FC01					12/08/2014 BACS		6,308.20	0.00	Y		6,308.20	R	31/08/2014
		63	1200	0	Sales Receipt				6,308.20	0.00 T9			6,308.20	-	
					6308.20 to SI 1	12/08/2014 O/Bal							6,308.20		
64	SR	FSS02					12/08/2014 BACS		3,339.90	0.00	Y		3,339.90	R	31/08/2014
		64	1200	0	Sales Receipt				3,339.90	0.00 T9			3,339.90	-	
					3339.90 to SI 2	12/08/2014 O/Bal							3,339.90		
65	SA	FSS02					18/08/2014 BACS		2,400.00	0.00	N		0.00	R	31/08/2014
		65	1200	0	Payment on Account				2,400.00	0.00 T9			0.00	-	
66	PP	ROS01					22/08/2014 BACS		4,350.00	0.00	Y		4,350.00	R	31/08/2014
		66	1200	0	Purchase Payment				4,350.00	0.00 T9			4,350.00	-	
					4350.00 to PI 5	22/08/2014 O/Bal							4,350.00		
67	PP	SS01					22/08/2014 BACS		16,868.92	0.00	Y		16,868.92	R	31/08/2014
		67	1200	0	Purchase Payment				16,868.92	0.00 T9			16,868.92	-	
					16868.92 to PI 59	22/08/2014 012012							16,868.92		
68	PA	WSL01					22/08/2014 BACS		5,000.00	0.00	N		0.00	R	31/08/2014
		68	1200	0	Payment on Account				5,000.00	0.00 T9			0.00	-	
69	PP	TKAS01					14/08/2014 201635		5,134.04	0.00	Y		5,134.04	R	31/08/2014
		69	1200	0	Purchase Payment				5,134.04	0.00 T9			5,134.04	-	
					3740.60 to PI 7	14/08/2014 O/Bal							3,740.60		
					1393.44 to PI 56	14/08/2014 INV635							1,393.44		
70	BP	1200					14/08/2014 201634		575.00	115.00	Y		690.00	R	31/08/2014
		70	7008	0	Advert				575.00	115.00 T1			690.00	N	
71	BP	1200					30/08/2014 201636		65.00	13.00	Y		78.00	N	
		71	7550	0	Thorpe Telephones				65.00	13.00 T1			78.00	N	
72	BR	1200					18/08/2014 94		331.67	66.33	Y		398.00	R	31/08/2014
		72	4003	0	Calculators				331.67	66.33 T1			398.00	N	
73	BR	1200					13/08/2014 Receipt		20,000.00	0.00	Y		20,000.00	R	31/08/2014
		73	2300	0	Bank loan received				20,000.00	0.00 T9			20,000.00	-	
74	JC	1200					27/08/2014 TRANS		15,000.00	0.00	Y		15,000.00	R	31/08/2014
		74	1200	0	Bank Transfer from current				15,000.00	0.00 T9			15,000.00	-	
75	JD	1210					27/08/2014 TRANS		15,000.00	0.00	Y		15,000.00	N	
		75	1210	0	Bank Transfer from current				15,000.00	0.00 T9			15,000.00	-	
76	BP	1200					24/08/2014 DD		72.60	14.52	Y		87.12	R	31/08/2014
		76	7701	0	PH Photocopeiers - maintenance				72.60	14.52 T1			87.12	N	
77	BR	1200					25/08/2014 STO		320.00	64.00	Y		384.00	R	31/08/2014
		77	4904	0	Harris Removals				320.00	64.00 T1			384.00	N	
78	JC	1200					02/08/2014 201633		50.00	0.00	Y		50.00	R	31/08/2014
		78	1200	0	Restore the petty cash account				50.00	0.00 T9			50.00	-	
79	JD	1230					02/08/2014 201633		50.00	0.00	Y		50.00	-	
		79	1230	0	Restore the petty cash account				50.00	0.00 T9			50.00	-	
80	CP	1230					02/08/2014 PC301		6.36	0.00	Y		6.36	-	
		80	7501	0	Stamps				6.36	0.00 T2			6.36	N	
81	CP	1230					05/08/2014 PC302		22.10	4.42	Y		26.52	-	
		81	6900	0	Cups for water machine				22.10	4.42 T1			26.52	N	
82	CP	1230					08/08/2014 PC303		6.92	1.38	Y		8.30	-	
		82	6900	0	Plants for reception				6.92	1.38 T1			8.30	N	
83	JD	4000					12/08/2014 017		64.80	0.00	Y		64.80	-	
		83	4000	0	Correction of error				64.80	0.00 T9			64.80	-	
84	JC	4003					12/08/2014 017		64.80	0.00	Y		64.80	-	
		84	4003	0	Correction of error				64.80	0.00 T9			64.80	-	

85	JD	3050				20/08/2014 018	350.00	0.00	Y	350.00	-	
		85	3050	0	Tanveer Mirza drawings		350.00	0.00 T9		350.00	-	
86	JC	5000				20/08/2014 018	350.00	0.00	Y	350.00	-	
		86	5000	0	Tanveer Mirza drawings		350.00	0.00 T9		350.00	-	
87	BP	1200				30/08/2014	40.00	0.00	Y	40.00	R	31/08/2014
		87	7901	0	Bank charges		40.00	0.00 T2		40.00	N	

for your notes

for your notes

for your notes

for your notes